GW00728087

The Lower Bure
from Great Yarmouth to Upton

Sheila Hutchinson

Front Cover Photograph:
The Stracey Arms Drainage Mill on the 24th April 2000.

Back Cover Photograph:
The Suspension Bridge over the River Bure connecting Great Yarmouth and Runham Vauxhall in 1938. Peter Allard Collection.

ISBN 9780954168360

Published
by
Sheila & Paul Hutchinson
7 Colman Avenue
Stoke Holy Cross
Norwich
Norfolk
NR14 8NA
England

Printed
By
RPD Litho Printers
Gorleston
Norfolk

PREFACE

It is with great pleasure that I have been asked to pen this forward for Sheila and Paul's new book on the River Bure between Great Yarmouth and Upton Dyke, their eighth publication in less than a decade. Their first publication concerned the Berney Arms and its people and memories of past times. Without this, much of its history of the Berney Arms would surely have been lost for forever. Who would have thought that a publication of a small and relatively unknown marshland hamlet would quickly sell out. This book ran to a second edition and its popularity was such that a newer book had to be published. This was Berney Arms Remembered and was published in 2003. Again, it proved very popular and its writings about a corner of Broadland virtually unwritten about by previous writers, together with considerable painstaking research into local families, buildings and windmills gave it high status in local bookshops.

Given the strength of Sheila's enthusiasm and local knowledge and Paul's dedication in researching old references, maps and photographs, further publications soon followed the first Berney Arms book.

The Halvergate Fleet: Past and Present appeared in 2001 and The Island (Haddiscoe Island) in 2002. Both sold out in a very short period of time. Sheila and Paul then turned their research to both Burgh Castle and Reedham, villages interlinked with the history of Berney Arms and the flat adjacent marshlands. Burgh Castle Remembered appeared in 2005 and Reedham Remembered the following year. A companion book Reedham Memories soon followed in 2007. All as expected proved very popular given the considerable effort both Sheila and Paul had put into producing additional books for this series.

For the researcher, much effort has been put in detailing local census records, tithe and enclosure maps and very importantly, involved people living in these areas and asking for their memories which would otherwise have probably been lost forever. This unique style has proved a winning formula and the new book on the River Bure from Great Yarmouth to Upton Dyke is no different. Having read through most of the draft write-up, there were many exciting details which were completely new to me. I'm sure the reader will also find this new publication well researched and full of information and together with its many photographs, some published for the first time, will be a welcome addition to the bookshelf.

Peter Allard.

UP THE NORTH RIVER. GREAT YARMOUTH.

An old postcard of an unidentified location on the North River, the alternative name for the River Bure.

INTRODUCTION

Land submergence and elevation thousands of years ago altered the coastline of East Anglia and the area now occupied by the marshes of the lower Bure, Yare and Waveney were once part of a shallow bay or estuary. At the time of the Roman occupation of Britain, Norfolk would have looked much like the map given below.

The gradual elevation of the land combined with the formation of a sandbank at what has become Great Yarmouth and the silting up of the estuary has created the rivers and marshlands. Embankment of the rivers probably began around the twelfth century and helped in the reclamation of the marshland. In the thirteenth century the sea level was about thirteen feet lower than it is today!

The River Bure enters the river Yare at TG518079 where on the right bank, ie the west side of the river is Runham Vauxhall and on the east side of the river is Great Yarmouth. The Bure is many miles in length extending well beyond the north-west boundary of the Broadland District. In a book of this size it is not possible to cover the whole river and we shall only be dealing with the lower reaches of the river from Great Yarmouth to Upton Mill.

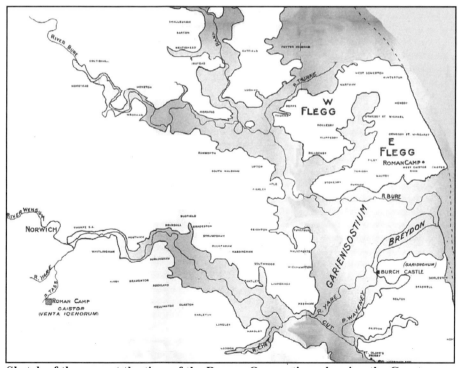

Sketch of the area at the time of the Roman Occupation, showing the Great Estuary.

The mouth of the Bure in July 1983 Peter Allard Collection.

Over the decades and centuries the maintenance of the river walls has been important to ensure that the reclaimed marshlands are not flooded by the river waters. The predicted rising sea levels, much discussed in recent years and resulting from Global Warming, mean it is essential that the river embankments are strengthened and raised, and work has been progressing along much of the river in recent years.

In recent months the Environment Agency have began to do flood defence improvements to the Right bank of the river between Acle Dyke and the Bure Mouth. The work involves strengthening and 'set back' of the floodbank and installation of erosion protection and new piling in some places.

Much of the land on either side of the river has been marshland used for grazing cattle, and in some cases sheep and horses, for several centuries. The drainage of the marshes was done with wind-pumps usually referred to as drainage windmills. Wind power was often replaced during the nineteenth century by steam engine pumps and then by diesel power, and eventually in the mid twentieth century by electric pumping stations. The river Bure has an abundance of old derelict, and sometimes restored, windpumps and many of these are featured in this short volume.

Top: Vessels unloading in January 1984 at John Lee Barber & Co. Peter Allard Collection.
Bottom: Derelict John Lee Barber & Co. silos at the Mouth of the Bure in February 2008. John Lee Barber & Co was listed as Grain Merchants in 1913 and as Corn & Cattle Food Merchants at Bowling Green Walk, North Quay in 1965.

RUNHAM VAUXHALL

On the west side of the river is Runham Vauxhall, originally a detached part of Runham parish. It was mainly agricultural and marshland and not very populated till the mid to late nineteenth century. The owner of most of the land here was at one time Robert Cory. Robert Cory owned some 66 acres in Runham detached in 1839 according to the Tithe Map and Apportionment. The Vauxhall Pleasure Gardens was located here near the mouth of the river, and here dancing, music concerts, illuminations and fireworks displays were held similar to those that occurred at the Vauxhall Pleasure Gardens in London.

Following the building of the Yarmouth Suspension Bridge and then later the Vauxhall Railway Station, which was built on the land to the south of the Pleasure Gardens, the area close to the river became more populated.

In August 1856 the Vauxhall Gardens and some 70 acres of agricultural and marsh land, referred to as 'The Ferry Farm', was put up for sale (NRO/Y/TC79/42). Most of the land was purchased and soon developed with housing and industry.

The 'night-soil' from the Yarmouth 'privies' was dumped in Runham Vauxhall during the nineteenth century by the 'honeycart' men.

In 1861 the population of Runham Vauxhall was 53 but by 1881 the population had grown to 606.

It once had two public houses, the Vauxhall Tavern and The Suspension Bridge Tavern, and in the late 1800s there were shops, marine stores, a school (built in 1879), a Foundry, a Tar and Chemical Works, and a Manure Works.

In the1890s Runham Vauxhall became part of the Great Yarmouth Borough and the Local Government Act of 1894 created Runham Vauxhall Civil Parish.

VAUXHALL RAILWAY STATION TG519081

This was built in 1844 when the Yarmouth to Norwich, via Reedham, line was built. It was built on the southern edge of the Vauxhall Pleasure Gardens on the west side of the river. On the Runham Tithe Map of 1839 this area was labelled as Gorleston. In 1911 the station was included in the newly created Parish of St. Mary, Southtown.

When the station was first built there was a dock created alongside leading from Breydon Water according to the Illustrated London News of 10th May 1845. This was to enable easy transfer of cargo and passengers between rail and boat.

There was once an icehouse near the station and in the 1920s the coal merchants Bessey and Palmer Ltd had a depot in the Station Yard. In the 1950s E.R. Newman was a coal merchant at the Station Yard and in the 1960s North Sea Coaling Co was a coal & coke merchants.

Some damage occurred to the station buildings during WWII.

The station was rebuilt and modernised in 1960.

Most of the sidings and engine shed fell into disuse after 1959 and were lost when the Asda supermarket was built in the late 1980s. Asda store opened in April 1989.

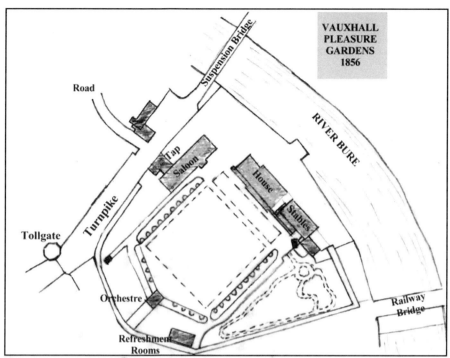

Top: Sketch of the Vauxhall Pleasure Gardens. Bottom: The Vauxhall Tavern. Peter Allard Collection.

THE VAUXHALL TAVERN TG520081

This pub was located on the Vauxhall Pleasure Gardens. In later years the address was given as Vauxhall Street, Station Yard. It was located opposite the present railway station car park.

It eventually closed in 1989 and was demolished in 1990.

On the Runham Tithe Map of 1839 the northern part of the Vauxhall Gardens was marked on area 351 and shown as occupied by John Symonds and owned by Robert Cory. Cory purchased the Runham Vauxhall estate in 1810. The southern part of the gardens was outside Runham detached parish and in the Southtown parish. The building which became known as the Vauxhall Tavern was not marked on the 1839 map, but the building, which was referred to as the House, in 1856, was the public house at that time and was the house of Ferry Farm.

It had a full licence according to the Gt. Yarmouth Licence Registers. Some owners listed in the old registers include: the **WYMONDHAM BREWERY**, it was conveyed to **MORGANS** on 11th May 1894; **BULLARDS,** and later **WATNEY MANN.**

It has been listed in various directories over the years with several different names and some of the earlier names include: The **VAUXHALL GARDENS, VAUXHALL GARDENS & BOWLING GREEN, VAUXHALL TAVERN, ROYAL VAUXHALL GARDENS, VAUXHALL REFRESHMENT ROOMS, RAILWAY REFRESHMENT ROOMS** and **VAUXHALL GARDENS HOTEL.**

When the Vauxhall Gardens was put up for sale 12th August 1856 it was described as:

Lot 19: The Vauxhall Gardens, Bowling Green, surrounded with Arbours, tastefully laid out Pleasure Grounds, also additional valuable Ground to be laid to Garden, of Land between the Railway Bridge and the Suspension Bridge down to the river (380 feet frontage), containing together 2a 0r 25p.

The House contains entrance hall, bar, large room divided by moveable partitions, three sitting rooms, nine sleeping rooms, kitchen, wash-house and dairy. Contiguous to the house are Ale and Porter Stores, Bottling Yard, Five-Stalled Stable with Loft over, boarded Stable, Shed and Yard.

A well-built Dancing Saloon 90 ft by 27 ft used occasionally as a skittle ground, with Stage at end, Tap and Porter Room facing the New road. The recently erected White brick Railway Refreshment Rooms immediately opposite and within a few yards of the Railway Station commanding the passenger business. This lot is now in the occupation of John Bartram, who is under notice to quit on the 10th October next.

The above mentioned Railway Refreshment Rooms became the site of the public house of later times.

The Pleasure Gardens stopped providing entertainment in about 1870 and the old house (Ferry Farm) became John Bly's foundry. In 1901 Ferry Farm House was occupied by William E. Mayes who was the manager of the ironworks. Most of the old pleasure gardens area was soon built on and the 1880s OS map shows several buildings here.

Occupier / Licensee	Notes /Comments	Dates
JOHN SYMONDS	Age 60 in 1841 census.	Prior to 1836
JOHN FRANKLIN		1845
EVADNE FRANKLIN		1850
PARKER BRADSTREET	age 37 in 1851	1851 - 1854
JOHN BARTRAM		1856 - 1869
WILLIAM BALLS		1869
JOHN H. BLY	& ironmonger. He later had a foundry here near the station at Ferry Farm in 1881.	1871
JOHN KEEBLE	Age 49 in 1881 census	1879 - 1883
JOHN BARTRAM		1888
WILLIAM THOMAS BLYTH		1890
ERNEST ALBERT HUNTER		by 1892
JAMES BENJAMIN GIBBS		20.10.1909
WALTER STONE		05.01.1917
PERCY OWEN STONE		07.04.1931
HAROLD DAVEY SEMMENCE		26.08.1941
WILLIAM GEORGE GREEN		24.10.1944
STANLEY JAMES WOOLSEY		06.04.1948
WILLIAM ALBERT BELLAMY		13.10.1958
CHARLES ARTHUR LEONARD COOPER		07.12.1964
RONALD HUTCHINSON		06.04.1966
RONALD EDMUND COOKE		09.02.1968
DORIS M COOKE		09.09.1971
JEAN & GORDON FREDERICK JAMES		09.12.1971

VAUXHALL BRIDGE.

The first bridge here was built in 1844/5 and was an iron girder bridge for pedestrians and horse-drawn trams. Later, in 1887, the bridge was modified / rebuilt to take heavier steam engine traffic. The trams stopped running in 1928 and in 1931 it took road traffic diverted from the Suspension Bridge. The bridge remains to this day, but it is currently a derelict Grade 11 listed building owned by Sustrans and only the pedestrian walkway / cycle path at the side is open, the main part being fenced off. The high water clearance for river traffic is 2.06 metre (6'9").

The Vauxhall Bridge in February 2008.

Sketch of the Remains of the Suspension Bridge from London Illustrated of 1845.

SUSPENSION BRIDGE.

On Faden's 1797 map and Bryant's 1826 map only a ferry was shown connecting Gt. Yarmouth to Runham Vauxhall. The marshes on the Runham Vauxhall side of the river had very few properties at that time. Robert Cory owned the land on the Runham side of the river and he owned the ferry. The Suspension Bridge Act of 1827 was passed and Cory had the bridge built and charged a toll for crossing the bridge.

Construction began in mid 1828 and the suspension bridge was opened in April 1829, and cost almost £4000, including the tollbooths at each end. It had octagonal toll houses at either end. After the railway station was built in 1844 the bridge was altered with the addition of pedestrian walkways on each side.

Made with iron chains attached to four iron plinths, it crossed the river Bure until it collapsed on 2nd May 1845. The collapse caused several hundred people to fall into the river, some reports said 79 of which drowned, mostly children.

On the 2nd of May 1845, Great Yarmouth was abuzz with excitement following the arrival of Cooke's Circus to the town. A publicity stunt was advertised: Nelson the Clown would sail from the bridge up the River Yare into the River Bure and through the Suspension Bridge in a washtub towed by four geese. The best place from which to view this spectacle was generally agreed to be the suspension bridge. Hundreds turned out, cramming themselves onto the bridge. When Nelson came into view, the crowd rushed to the side he was approaching from. The bridge became unbalanced, the suspension chains on one side broke and the bridge collapsed, plunging everyone on it, the majority of whom were children, into the river. All available boats rushed to the scene and many spectators were saved, but tragically many men, woman and children perished in the river that day.

A temporary bridge was erected a few weeks after the disaster.

The replacement bridge of 1847 continued to be called the Suspension Bridge. The replacement bridge was an 88 feet span Bowstring wrought iron bridge. The arches were made as 18 inch diameter riveted tubes. It had vertical suspenders of 2" x2" x5/16" with diagonals made from 1.5 and 2 inch diameter bars. The cross girders spanned 15 feet and supported a timber deck.

From 1931 traffic was diverted from the Suspension Bridge to the Vauxhall Bridge but the Suspension bridge remained open for pedestrians. Tank barriers were erected on the bridge and during the war years the barriers were also across the pedestrian walkway. The bridge remained unused thereafter and in 1953 it was demolished by Elliot and Hicks of Great Yarmouth who tendered a price of £300 to remove the derelict bridge.

The gatekeeper at the Bure Bridge Tollgate in 1841 on the Runham side was Charles Bailey, 57.

On the Runham Vauxhall side of the river the 1881 census lists James John Royal, age 54, as the Toll Proprietor, and John Tripp, age 76, was listed at Toll Gate House as the Toll Collector. In 1883 Catherine Tripp, John's widow, was the toll collector. She was also listed as the Toll Collector in 1891.

Two sketches of the Suspension Bridge disaster of 1845. The North West tower and the octagonal tollbooth on the Yarmouth side of the river are shown.

The Second Suspension Bridge.
Top: 1908 looking upriver, from Derek Williams.
Bottom: 1938 looking downriver.
Peter Allard collection.

In 1901 the toll collector at the Gate house in Runham Vauxhall was Herbert Gaut, age 36

The Tolls for the bridge were abolished in March 1920. The Toll house on the Vauxhall side was demolished in 1953.

The third bridge was the **Calender-Hamilton Bridge,** a temporary girder bridge built to replace the second bridge over the river Bure. Built in 1951/52 at a cost of £40,000, and opened on the 5th January 1953, it was intended to last for only ten years. It remained until March 1972, when the present four lane Bure Road Bridge was opened. The present bridge clearance at high water is 2.13m (7 ft.).

The Second Suspension Bridge and North Tower.

ACLE NEW ROAD

The New Road from the Suspension Bridge to Acle was built in 1831. Prior to its construction the road to Acle from Great Yarmouth was via Caister and was about 3 and a half miles longer.

Norfolk Chronicle - 23rd April 1831

'On Wednesday, the 13th inst. pursuant to advertisement, the Acting Trustees of the new Acle and Yarmouth Turnpike, with John Prentice Esq. their chairman, the Rev. Charles Penrice, H. N. Borroughs Esq. T. H. Batcheler, Esq. R. Cory Esq. C. Nichols

16

Esq. W. W. Branford Esq. and other gentlemen, met at the Suspension Bridge, on the North Quay, to walk over the line of road, and inspect the progress of the works. - It appears that the bridge over Tunstall Boat Dyke is complete; the arches and trunks over Land Spring Drains, the Mill Drains, and the entire line of road formed, and that to complete it, previously to its being opened to the public, the materials (which are broken stones and shingles) remain to be laid on, and these are actually prepared, and landed over the river wall, whence they will be conveyed in boats down the dykes to different parts of the roads. - The Trustees were accompanied by Mr. Isaac Lenny, of Norwich, the company's surveyor, by Mr. Thorold, the Contractor, and other gentlemen and the Trustees were pleased to express their gratification at the manner the works were going on, and afterwards an excellent dinner, provided at Acle Queen's Head, in Mr. England's best style. - perhaps it is not generally known, that the saving of distance from Acle to Yarmouth will be three miles and five furlongs, and a great advantage of the project is, that by means of the branches, a large tract of the country will be laid open to Yarmouth, which has hitherto been nearly excluded for a great part of the year, on account of the distance of roads by a very circuitous route. In addition to the satisfaction which the trustees feel at the progress of the works, the shareholders have the gratification of knowing that they will receive ample interest on the principal money, invested so judiciously, and with so much public spirit in this useful undertaking.'

TURNPIKE TOLL ROADS

Tollgates were erected along the Acle New Road, one at the Yarmouth end in Runham detached at TG515089, one at the Acle Tunstall parish boundaries at TG423096 and a further tollgate near the Stracey Arms at the junction of Branch Road with the New Road.

In 1841 Samuel Scales, age 15, was listed as the Tollgate Keeper in Acle.

In 1851, at entry no. 3, for Tunstall we have listed John Ward, age 75, Turnpike Gate Keeper, born Stokesby. This dwelling was a building next to the Stracey Arms where Branch Road, leading to Halvergate, joined the Acle New Road.

The Turnpike Toll House at the Yarmouth end of the New Road was on the south side of the road in Runham detached parish and close to the bend in the road. It was shown on the 1839 Runham Tithe map at area 347 and listed as owned and occupied by the 'Trustees of New Turnpike'. In the Runham census of 1851 entry 25 is the Tollgate and lists John Powley, age 35, as the toll collector. The building was marked on the c1880 OS map but not labelled. This location on the 1907 and 1938 OS maps was labelled as '**STRAWBERRY FARM**'. Mrs Andrews was listed as the occupant of Strawberry Farm in 1938 and John Rouse in 1948 and 1963. The road here was later altered, and the rerouted road was to the south of the old turnpike house location.

The Calender-Hamilton Bridge being dismantled in May 1972. From the Peter Allard Collection.
Top: looking towards Yarmouth with Lacon's Stores in the centre picture.
Bottom: Looking towards Runham Vauxhall. The steel lighter 'Birch' is being used to support the bridge structure.

Calender-Hamilton Bridge and the earlier Suspension bridge on left. The Buildings opposite on North Quay had several pubs at one time.

Steamboat Pride of the Yare upstream of the Suspension Bridge with passengers. From Peter Allard Collection.

The Old Toll booth for the Suspension Bridge on Yarmouth North Quay. This became known as the Round House and was used before WWI by Robert Palmer, a bootmaker, and later by Louis George Dyble also a bootmaker. Peter Allard Collection.

Sailing Shrimpers in about 1912 moored upriver of the Vauxhall Bridge at Runham Vauxhall. Peter Allard Collection.

SUSPENSION BRIDGE TAVERN

This is located at 25 BRIDGE ROAD, Runham Vauxhall on the west side of the river almost opposite the White Swan. It was not marked on the 1839 Tithe Map of Runham, or on the 1856 sale particulars when the Runham land was sold.

This was listed as a Beer house then later had a Full Licence in the Gt. Yarmouth Licence Registers.

The Gt. Yarmouth Licence Registers list some of the owners as: MARY ANN SMITH, LACONS in 1928, and then WHITBREAD.

Suspension Bridge Tavern.

Occupant / licensee	Comments	Date
	NOT LISTED	1854
WILLIAM SMITH	He was listed only as boat owner, fish merchant & curer in 1868. Age 59 in 1881, born Ludham, fish merchant. In 1883 listed as beerhouse. He had one of the largest wherries, the 80 tons wherry 'Wonder', built in the yard next to the pub in 1878 by James Benns and Thomas Cassey.	1868

Mrs MARY ANN SMITH	Wife of above, age 45 in 1881.	by 1888
ELEANOR SOPHIA ELLIS	.	05.02.1908
JAMES WALTER CLARKE	.	07.04.1908
WILLIAM ROBERT GEORGE	.	07.01.1916
GEORGE BUCKSEY	.	04.01.1921
EMILY BUCKSEY	.	30.05.1922
WILLIAM MINISTER BURRELL	.	03.04.1923
MAUD SARAH BURRELL	.	10.03.1950
GILBERT THOMAS WALDEN	.	06.07.1954
PERCY ROY ALLEN	.	21.04.1959
Mr & Mrs SAMUEL MORGAN	.	01.11.1960
CLIFFORD HARRY SILLIS	.	25.05.1972
JAMES STACKHOUSE	.	07.12.1972
JO PACKHAM		Currently

Suspension Bridge Tavern in 2008.

The Acle New Road Bridge in 2008.

The White Swan Public House and North West Tower in 2008.

Top: Bure Railway Bridge in December 1976.
Bottom: Railway Shed at Vauxhall Station in March 1975.
Peter Allard Collection.

BURE RAILWAY BRIDGE TG520086

This metal girder bridge carried the railway line from Beech Station across the river Bure. The line then went along an embankment crossing over the Yarmouth Norwich line and then across the Breydon Viaduct and onto Gorleston.
The bridge was built circa 1900 and was demolished in the late 1970s.

The Bure Railway Bridge in 1977 before demolition.

RIVERSIDE INDUSTRY IN RUNHAM VAUXHALL

Runham Vauxhall being on the river had many people in the later part of the nineteenth century who were involved with boat building and river transport. Some of those listed living in Runham Vauxhall in the 1881 census include: **Watermen**: William Benns, Arthur W. Benns, Samuel Nichols, Robert Smith and Robert Carr; **Boat Builders**: Thomas Cassey, George Puttuck, Fred Puttuck, William S. Dye and John Read. Benjamin Benns was another boat-builder listed in 1891 and 1913.

Many others were involved with fishing related products.

There were Manure, Chemical and Tar Works developed in Runham Vauxhall near to the river.

After the construction of the railway and the station many of the people living at Runham Vauxhall were railway employees.

A Thomas Parmenter was listed in 1868 and 1875 as a 'Fish Manure & Timber Merchant' and Jonas Barnes was listed as a 'Fish Manure Merchant' near the Suspension Bridge. George Barnes and sons was listed in 1881, 1916 and in 1933 as 'Fish Curers' and 'Fish manure manufacturer & merchant' and as 'Salt Merchant' in 1913. Much of the fish manure would have been taken by wherry from here to be used for fertilising the farmlands up river. (Note: Fish manure is made from fish offal and the fish carcasses discarded during processing for human consumption. The manure is better if the oil has been removed, as then it is quicker acting. Fish manure usually contains sufficient nitrogen and phosphates for most crops, but practically no potash.)

George Archer, after whom Archers Road was named, was listed on North River Road before WWI as another Manure Merchant and in 1927 he was listed as 'Fish Manure and Salt Merchant'. On Archer's Road in 1913 A & M Smith was listed as Fish Canners & Preservers'

Benjamin Ingham was a shrimper listed in 1913 and 1927

The **RUNHAM TAR Works** (TG519089), on North River Road, was shown on the 1880s and 1928 OS maps, and were occupied in 1869 and 1883 by J.J. Blott & Co who was Tar distillers and manufacturers, and chemists. There were no buildings marked at this location, area 370, on the Tithe map of the 1839 or on the 1856 sale particulars. The British Gas Light Co Ltd took over these premises in Runham Vauxhall and was listed in 1892 and 1938 as Tar distillers and manufacturing chemists. The North Sea Coaling Co. Ltd. and the Gorleston Coaling Co Ltd were also located here in later years. Later the Great Yarmouth Coach Works was located near here on North River Road.

The **MANURE Works** (TG519089), also on North River Road, was shown on the 1880s and 1938 OS maps. There were no buildings marked here on area 367 on the Tithe map of the 1839 or the 1856 sale particulars.

This was in 1875 and 1892 run by Bayley & Sutton and listed as 'Chemical & Artificial Manure Manufacturers & Merchants' and 'Vitriol & Manure Manufacturers'.

Later Prentice Brothers Ltd (Chemical) was listed here as Manure Manufacturers in 1913 and 1922. In 1933 and 1938 the company was listed as Fison, Packard & Prentice Ltd. Fertiliser manufacturers.

In 1952 and 1965 the works were occupied by Case & Steward Ltd who was compound fertiliser manufacturers.

Another manure works was located at about TG515090 and was listed in 1892 as Robinson Pattinson's Guano Works, manufacturers of fish and guano manure. The roadway leading to the site of the works is today called Pattinsons Road.

Others found in Runham Vauxhall include Ambrose Powley who was listed as a maltster in 1881 and John Bly of Ferry Farm House was an ironmonger and had a **foundry** near the railway station. This was later listed in 1913 as the Great Yarmouth Iron Works & Foundry Co. Ltd. on Bridge Road.

Tunbridge & Sons were Tallow merchants on Archers Road in the 1950s and also were listed as Dripping Manufacturers. Moody Bros Ltd. were Fish Curers on Sidegate Road in the 1950s and The Gorleston Coaling Co. Ltd. had a depot on North River Road in the 1960s.

RIVERSIDE INDUSTRIES BY THE BURE IN YARMOUTH

Many shops, stores, public houses and other businesses have been located along the Bure riverside over the years.

The short cobbled road on the Yarmouth side of the river called 'Lime Kiln Walk' is indicative of a Lime Kiln in the vicinity in earlier times.

On the 1848 Tithe Map of Gt. Yarmouth a Philip Nuthall was listed as the occupier of areas 107 Shed, Sawpit & Yard, 108 Warehouses & Yards, 109 Old Town Cottages & Yard and 110 House, Garden and **Lime Kiln**. This was the area adjacent to the old town walls North WestTower. Philip Nuthall was also listed as a Brewer and Maltster in 1845. William Dye was listed at Lime Kiln Wharf, North Quay as a boatbuilder in 1892.

Yarmouth Refuse destructor ruins after WWII. Colin Tooke Collection.

Paget & Sons were Brewers and Maltsters on North Quay near the River Bure in front of the Vauxhall Bridge and were listed in 1845. The Brewery here was started in the 1730s as Browne's Brewery, became Fisher's Brewery, and in 1794 it was taken over by Patteson and Thompson. Paget bought the brewery in 1804 and sold it in 1845 to Steward & Patteson. In 1847 it was sold to the Railway Company and it was demolished to make way for the railway line coming from the quayside and the Vauxhall Bridge.

On the Yarmouth side of the Bure there was a **maltings** next to the river and which at one time belonged to Lacon's Brewery. Their brewery stores were on the opposite side of North Quay roadway. **LACON'S BREWERY** was originally founded in 1640 by Jeffery Ward and acquired by a Mr. Lacon in 1760. Whitbread purchased a 20% share holding in 1957, and later Whitbread & Co Ltd took over in November 1965 at a reported purchase price of £3,200,000. The Brewery closed in February 1968. The brewery stores was the last building to survive. It was demolished in 1997.

There was a **Tar Works** on the riverside at about TG522091 marked on

Smith's Potato Crisps Ltd., 127 Caister Road. Colin Tooke Collection.

the 1881 and later OS maps. The short roadway here is still called Tar Works Road. On the 1848 tithe map a house was located here which was occupied by Thomas Birch. The land here was at that time owned by The Children's Hospital.

On the riverside and on the north side of Tar Works Road there was the **Refuse Destructor** which was marked on the circa 1907 and 1938 OS maps. This was built in 1902 and damaged during WWII in 1942 and eventually demolished.

Smiths Crisps had a Factory on Caister Road from 1935 till 1983. It was demolished in May 1985.

There was also a **slaughter house** on Caister Road, **Frosdicks** near the Bure Hotel. This was started by Henry Frosdick and later taken over by Arthur Frosdick. The 1969 directory lists A J Frosdick as Horse Slaughterers both here and at Market Gates.

Frosdick's Slaughter House in the 1970s. Colin Tooke Collection.

GREAT YARMOUTH PUBS

There were five public houses in the buildings on the Gt. Yarmouth North Quay near the river Bure and close to the Suspension Bridge, all but one of which have long been demolished, some more recently to make way for the new road layout when the new road bridge over the river was built. These were the North Star, the North Tower, the Norwich Arms, the Lord Collingwood and the White Swan.

NORTH STAR

This was a beerhouse located on the SW corner of Row 9, North Quay to Fullers Hill. It was referred to Compensation on 03.03.1933. The Licence expired on 07.07.1933, and the pub closed in 1933. The licence register give the owners as **W. H. BERSEY** of Gt. Yarmouth, but it was leased to Lacon & Co. **LACON & Co**. became the owners by 1928

Licencee / Occupant	Date
EDWARD BARNES	1858 - 1886
JOHN JAMES GREEN	1890
GEORGE THAXTER	by 1900
WILLIAM FOLKES	06.07.1906
THOMAS HENRY HIPGRAVE	17.08.1917
WILLIAM JAMES HARMER	02.01.1923
ALICE MAY HARMER	26.05.1925

NORTH TOWER
Originally a BEERHOUSE and then later had a FULL LICENCE. It was located at 16A North Quay, Row 8. The Beerhouse licence was given up 18.11.1904 in consideration of a new licence granted to the Golf Arms, and a full licence was granted 18.11.1904 by way of removal from the Norwich Arms and on condition of surrender from the **Tomlinson Arms**. It finished trading on 16th August 1966. It was owned by **LACON & Co** in 1903 then later became a **WHITBREAD** house.

Licensee / Occupant	Date
Mrs. FANNY HILL NEWMAN	by 1903
THOMAS QUINTON	18.11.1904
FANNY HILL NEWMAN	13.01.1905
ALFRED EDWARD WALKER	13.08.1915
KATHLEEN ADA WALKER	02.03.1917
ALFRED EDWARD WALKER	10.08.1920
HARRY BURGESS	22.10.1940
ISAAC ARTHUR CHAPLIN	12.12.1944
EMMA ELIZABETH CHAPLIN	05.02.1965
JOHN HODGSON	01.11.1966

NORWICH ARMS
The address has been given as 15 or16 North Quay. It had a full licence. It CLOSED in 1904. The licence was surrendered on 18.11.1904 in consideration of licence granted to the North Star. Some owners from the licence registers are **STEWARD & Co.** and **LACON & Co.** in 1903.

Licensee / Occupant	Date
JOHN LAWS	1845

MARY FUTTER (?)	1850
GEORGE MASON	1854
JOHN PLANE	1856 - 1890
HARRY FEEK	1896 - 1900
THOMAS QUINTON	by 1903
ARTHUR GILBERT RAYNER	21.08.1903
JAMES NEWMAN	15.04.1904

LORD COLLINGWOOD
6 LAUGHING IMAGE CORNER NORTH QUAY.
The owners were LACON & Co. in 1819. It was previously known as **The Wherry**.
It had a full licence and the last licence was granted 02.02.1904, and it closed in 1905.
The Licence was given up for the THREE TUNS in Gorleston in 1905.

Licensee	Date
JOHN KIRK	1819
JOHN BESSEY age 53 in 1851	1824 - 1871
ROBERT BESSEY	1875
SAMUEL WARNER	1879
JAMES BARBER	1883 - 1888
JAMES NEWMAN	by 1892

WHITE SWAN Public House.
This is located at 1 North Quay in Gt. Yarmouth on the east side of the river and
survives to this day. It is believed to have been built originally in the 18th century and
rebuilt in the 19th century. It was given a makeover in May 1979 costing £21,000.

Some owners from the Licence Registers were: PAGET & Co. in 1819. It
was conveyed by Samuel Paget & Others to MORSE, STEWARD, FINCH &
PATTESON on 23.08.1845 and later became a WATNEY MANN pub.

Occupant/ Licensee	Comments	Dates
BENJAMIN MUNFORD		1819 - 1830
JAMES MUNFORD		1836
BENJAMIN MUNFORD		1839 - 1845
ABIGAIL JEX		1850
RICHARD G PARMENTER	Porter Merchant, 1851, age 39	1854 - 1863
GEORGE CROWE		1865 - 1869
THOMAS EMPSON		1875 - 1883
GEORGE CROWE		1888 - 1890
Mrs. MARY ANN CROWE		1892

WILLIAM PARMENTER		by 1896
ANGELINA CROWE		04.03.1924
ADA FLORENCE PARNELL		21.07.1925
WILLIAM BALDRY TAMMIS		10.11.1925
JOHN JOSEPH ABBOTT		05.11.1929
WILLIAM BALDRY TAMMIS		07.04.1931
WILLIAM KERRY BURTON		13.12.1938
FLORENCE EILEEN BURTON		24.10.1939
WILLIAM KERRY BURTON		23.10.1945
FREDERICK ERNEST NICHOLAS		09.03.1951
ALAN THURNE WILLIAMS		10.02.1956
STANLEY WILKINSON		09.02.1968

Steam Ship 'Queen of the Broads', full of day trippers, heading upriver between the Vauxhall Bridge and the Suspension Bridge in July 1971. The skipper at that time was Walter Rudd. The vessel was built at Cobholm Island in 1889 for Thomas Bradley, increased in length in 1896, and broken up in 1976. Peter Allard Collection.

White Swan and North West Tower.

North West Tower circa 1870. Peter Allard Collection.

Trading wherries laying alongside the White Swan public house and the North West Tower circa 1896. Peter Allard Collection.

The Wroxham Belle was a regular sight on the Bure working as a diesel powered river bus capable of carrying 200 passengers. Here it is shown at Great Yarmouth on the Yare near the Haven Bridge in 1937. It was built in 1936 for the Yarmouth and Gorleston Steamboat Company and was built to pass under the low Vauxhall and Suspension bridges. Peter Allard Collection.

OTHER PUBS IN GREAT YARMOUTH NEAR THE RIVER

Several other pubs existed close to the River Bure and include the following.

LORD NELSON

This was located at 85 NORTH QUAY

This building still exists on the corner of Lime Kiln Walk and North Quay and was built in 1895.

An earlier building with this name existed. The Address was given as 24 North Quay in 1822. **LACON & Co** was given as the owners in 1824 and later it was a **WHITBREAD** house.

The pub closed in about 1975 and then re-opened as `**DE REMO**', an Italian Restaurant in October 1975. It later became a Seafood Restaurant in the 1990s

Seafood Restaurant, once the Lord Nelson, in 2008.

Licensee	Comments	Date
WILLIAM FODDER		1819
JUDITH FODDER		1824 - 1839
RICHARD PARMENTER		1844 - 1845
WILLIAM CUTTING	age 38 in 1851	1850 - 1854
BENJAMIN JOHN BESSEY	& railway carrier 1861 Eel fisherman 1883	1863 - 1879
ALBERT W. BECKETT		1883
J W BECKETT		1886
RICHARD G. READ		1888 - 1890
HARRY FEEK		1892
ARTHUR GALLEHAWK		c.1900
ETHEL GALLEHAWK		06.07.1906

FREDERICK WILLIAM LOCK		12.10.1906
WILLIAM GEORGE BURTON		13.08.1915
FLORENCE BURTON		07.01.1916
ARTHUR CHARLES GREEN		21.07.1925
FRANK CLEMENT ELMER		10.05.1938
DENNIS PATRICK BYRNE		10.05.1955
NIGEL FREDERICK HUGGETT		08.09.1964
RAYMOND CHARLES GEORGE POULSON		12.12.1968

BOWLING GREEN

This was a Lacon's house located at NORTH QUAY near the junction of the Bure and the Yare and on BOWLING GREEN WALK. It closed circa 1900.

It has also been known as the **HORSE PACKET, SOVEREIGN BOWLING GREEN,** The **SOVEREIGN STEAM PACKET & BOWLING GREEN, ROYAL SOVEREIGN BOWLING GREEN, SOVEREIGN STEAM PACKET,** and **RAILWAY BOWLING GREEN.**

Licensee	Notes	Date
JOSEPH PIGG		1819 - 1824
EDMUND BAMMANT		1830 - 1839
WILLIAM PARMENTER		1845
THOMAS PARMENTER	age 26 in 1851	1850 - 1865
WILLIAM GEORGE PARMENTER	also a boat builder	1869
FREDERICK SILVERS BALDRY		1875 - 1877
JOHN CHRISTMAS		1883 - 1886
WILLIAM BEAMISH GREEN		1888
HERBERT EDWARD PYE		1890
JOHN LONG		1892

PRINCESS ALEXANDRA

Located at 2 Lime Kiln Walk this was a beerhouse run by Robert Bessey around 1856 to 1871.

PRINCESS AUGUSTA CUTTER

This was located on NORTH QUAY near the North West Tower and just outside the Town Wall. The owners were PAGET & Co in 1824. It is not listed in any of the White's or Kelly's directories so may have lost its licence before 1836.

Licensee		Date
RICHARD PARMENTER		1824
MATILDA MANSHIP		1830

BURE HOTEL

This pub was located on the Caister Road. It was built on the site of Fowlers Camp and opened in 1939. It had a full licence and was a Steward & Patteson house and later became a Watney Mann house.

It closed in 1985 and was demolished in 1986.

The Bure Hotel, March 1977. Peter Allard Collection.

Licensee	Dates	Comments
Elizabeth Rachel Rose Talbot	12 Dec 1939	Some damage in WWII
John Guy Talbot	11 Dec 1945	
Arthur Charles Wiseman	5 Dec 1950	
John Edmund Symonds	4 Dec 1951	
Helen Irene Iwaw Symonds	5 Feb 1954	
Wilfred Frederick Ward	4 Feb 1966	

Edward Kendle Thackery	30 May 1967	
John Austin Philips & Colin Roy Coe	9 Feb 1968	
Nicholas Stuart Prior	20 July 1969	
Bernard Frederick Grimmer	22 July 1971	
Arthur Henry Pinnell	7 Sept 1972	
George Dolman	1976	
Albert Smith	1981	

**The wherry 'Gleaner' at Great Yarmouth Yacht Station in 1939.
Peter Allard Collection.**

TOWN WALL

In 1261 Henry III granted the town of Great Yarmouth leave to build a town wall. The wall had 18 towers and 10 gates and was not completed till 1391. The tower which still stands near the White Swan was the North West Tower of the town wall.

YARMOUTH YACHT STATION

This is on the left bank of the river a short distance upriver from the White Swan public house. In the early nineteenth century pleasure wherries could be hired here. Nat Burcham ran the station in the 1950s. Today the **Yacht Station** is run by the Broads Authority whose quay attendants are called Rangers.

YACHTING STATION,
GT YARMOUTH.

The Yarmouth Yacht Station circa 1910. Peter Allard Collection.

PORT OF YARMOUTH MARINA

This is the last safe mooring place on the river till the Stracey Arms. Now called Marina Key's, it is located at TG522098 near Bure Park.

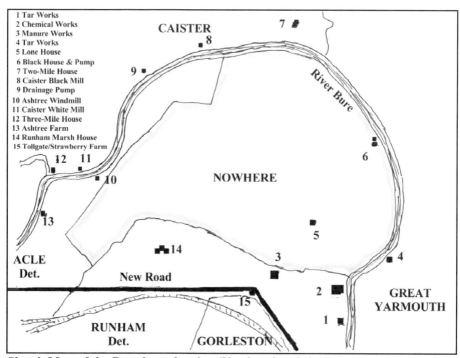

1 Tar Works
2 Chemical Works
3 Manure Works
4 Tar Works
5 Lone House
6 Black House & Pump
7 Two-Mile House
8 Caister Black Mill
9 Drainage Pump
10 Ashtree Windmill
11 Caister White Mill
12 Three-Mile House
13 Ashtree Farm
14 Runham Marsh House
15 Tollgate/Strawberry Farm

Sketch Map of the Bure loop showing 'Nowhere' and the location of some of the places mentioned in the text.

NOWHERE

In the 1869 Kelly's directory '**Nowhere**' was said to be a parish which had a population of 16 in 1861, and included the extra parochial parishes of Skeetholme, Fordholme and Stargap. The location of 'Nowhere' is in the Bure loop and is bounded on the east and north-east by the river, on the south by Runham Vauxhall and Runham detached, and on the west by Acle detached. Samuel Barnett Cory, solicitor and farmer, was given as the principal landowner here at that time. 'Nowhere' was annexed to Acle Parish under the provision of the Assessment Act of 1862.

In the 1845 directory Fordholme and Skeetholme were said to be 484 acres of salt marshes belonging to the Dean & Chapter of Norwich and let to the farmers of the adjacent parishes.

In the 1883 directory Nowhere was said to be an area of 484 acres and a Charles Jecks leased 267 acres.

Much of the land here in the twentieth century was bought by Charlie Wharton.

LONE HOUSE TG 518092

Lone House on 16 April 1972 in 'Nowhere' from Peter Allard Collection.

This dwelling was located in **Nowhere** and was shown on the 1880s and 1913 OS maps as Lone House. On the 1930 map it was called **White House Farm**.

The 1848 Acle Tithe map does not provide any information about the properties here and it is difficult to decipher which are the properties in Nowhere from the Acle census returns.

Some *possible* occupants from the census returns are:

1901 entry 206, Near Runham Vauxhall: William Golder, 58, stockman on Marshes.

1891 entry 213: William Golder, 48, marshman.

1881 entry 11, Farmhouse Nowhere: uninhabited.

1871 entry 8: Near Yarmouth Nowhere: John Smith, 43, labourer.

Henry Bailey was listed as a farmer in Acle (near Yarmouth) in the1916 and 1933 directories and was probably living here.

Fred Hewitt was a later occupant here, moving here in 1943 from Seven Mile House on the River Yare. The Hewitt family were here till 1966 and were the last occupants of the house. David Hewitt, one of Fred's sons, recalls that he went to Runham Vauxhall School and later to the Hospital School in Gt. Yarmouth.

BLACK HOUSE PUMP TG521097

A Draining Pump, or Pump House, and dwelling were shown on the 1880s, 1907 and 1951 OS maps on the west side of river. This was located in the area once known as '**Nowhere**', which was listed in the Acle detached parish census returns.

40

This pump was a steam engine drainage pump. No mill or pump was shown here on the 1797, 1826, and the 1996 maps.

The dwelling here was sometimes referred to as '**Black House**'.

Some *possible* entries from the Acle census returns are:

1901 unoccupied. 1891 uninhabited.

1881 entry 10: Samuel Cooper, marshman.

1871 entry 9, Black House New Road: Samuel Cooper, 56, marshman.

'Picky' Ernest Durrant and family were here at one time.

TWO MILE HOUSE TG5175 1031

This is shown on the north side of the river in West Caister parish on the 1880s OS map. It was marked as 'Marsh Farm' on the 1907 OS map.

This was shown on the 1797 and 1826 maps and the 1st edition OS map. This was marked on the Tithe map, circa 1840, at area 361 as 'Cottage & Gardens', owned by Sarah Scott & others and occupied by George Everitt.

The house was demolished in the 1970s.

Bonds Mill circa 1946. Colin Tooke Collection.

CAISTER BLACK MILL TG5123 1020

This was shown on the 1826 map on the north side of the river in 'West' Caister Parish. On the earlier 1797 map it was shown as '**Drain Wind Mill**'.

A mill was also marked here on the circa 1840 Tithe Map at area 368 and was labelled as '**Steam Engine Yard**'. It was owned by Sarah Scott & others and was occupied by George Everitt.

On the 1880s OS map it was shown as '**Draining Pump**'. It was not shown on the 1907 OS map but a 'boat house' was marked here! The 1951 OS map shows a '**Pump House**' here.

Rex Wailes listed this as '**Caister on Bure Mill**' in 1956, and A.C. Smith indicated this as "Old site with no remains" in 1989 and says there had been a tower mill here.

Nothing is shown here on the 1996 OS map.

The windmill here was replaced in about 1841 by a steam pump, which drove a scoopwheel and was known as '**BOND'S MILL**'.

The Bond family were at the Castle Farm in West Caister for many years:
(1836 directory: William Mayes Bond, 1854 directory John Mayes Bond, 1864 directory: William Mayes Bond, 1881 census: Mark Bond, 48, Farmer.)

The drainage pump was operated for a time by George Dyble and the pump finished working in about 1936.

DRAINING PUMP TG5090 1008
A 'Draining Pump' is shown on 1880s OS map on north side of river in Caister on Sea Parish at this location. No mill or pump was shown here on the 1797, 1826, and the Tithe Map of circa 1840. It is probable that this was a steam drainage pump.

On the 1907 OS map only a boat house is marked at this location!

ELM FARM HOLLOW POST MILL TG507111

Elm Hill Mill. Peter Allard Collection.

42

This was about ½ mile north of the river and close to Elm Farm in West Caister. It was shown on the 1880s OS map as a draining pump.

Rex Wailes says this was a hollow post mill with a plunger, possibly made by Whitmore & Binyon, and had twin weather vanes.

Colin Tooke says it was owned by the Kittle family at Elm Farm and stopped working in the late 1920s. The Kittle family was listed as farmers here in the 1836 and later directories and Joseph Kittle was listed as owner and occupier of several areas on the Tithe Map of circa 1840.

NEW ROAD MARSH FARM TG510091

New Road Marsh Farm, Runham detached, April 1984, from Peter Allard Collection.

Located in Runham detached it is shown on the 1880s OS map without a label, but is marked as Marsh Farm on later maps.

The 1839 Tithe Map for Runham Detached indicates buildings here on area 340 and gives the owner / occupier of areas 331 to 346 as Edward Ames. The buildings are not detailed in the Apportionment and area 340 is listed only as pasture.

Bryant's 1826 map indicates a 'marsh house' near here and close to Breydon Water, but Faden's earlier map of 1797 shows nothing here.

The 1841 Runham census lists an entry as Extra Parochial for William Moss, age 36, marsh farmer, and he is probably living here. (He may be related to William Moss who at that time was at AshTree Farm.)

The 1891 Runham Vauxhall census returns have George Laycock, age 66, living at entry 30, 'Amies Farm (Marsh Farm)'

The 1901 Runham census also lists as entry 67 Acle New Road; George Laycock, age 75, Dairyman / Farmer. Laycock was also listed in 1904 as a cowkeeper.

A Mr Henry Bailey was listed as a dairyman in Runham Vauxhall in 1908 and may have been here. A later occupant here was Mr Drake.

Although still marked on the 1996 OS map the buildings here were demolished in 1986.

CAISTER WHITE MILL TG506096

This was shown on the 1826 map on the north side of the river, with the name White Mill, in 'West' Caister Parish. It was marked on the Tithe map, circa 1840, but was not shown on 1797 map. It was shown as **Draining Pump** on 1880s OS map at this *approximate* location, on the 1907 OS map as a '**Windpump**', on the 1929 map as a 'draining pump', and on the 1951 map as '**Engine House**'.

On the Tithe map it was shown at the junction of areas 396, 394 and 393. Area 393 was owned by John Edward Lacon and the others by Thomas Reeve Daniel. The footings of the old mill were exposed in 2007 when work on the river bank was being carried out.

Colin Tooke says that a steam pump was built here around 1905 by E W England in a brick and slate engine house. It had a locomotive type boiler and could lift up to 6000 gallons per minute. It also drained the levels which had been connected to Bond's mill from about 1936 after a new dyke had been cut and Bond's mill stopped working. The pump worked till about 1946 when the electric pumps took over the drainage of the marshes. Harry Smith of 3 Mile House worked the pump for a time.

In Mautby Rememberance Samuel Howard says this was originally a wooden windpump that discharged into Pickerill Holme. It was however closer to the river than Pickerill Holme and probably discharged into the Bure.

AC Smith suggests there was a hollow post mill originally.

PICKERILL HOLME

This is a Dyke forming the boundary between the Mautby and West Caister Parishes and enters the river Bure on the north side, near to THREE MILE HOUSE. It runs toward Caister Castle and was probably navigable by small boats in days gone by.

A sluice is shown on the 1880s OS map where Pickerill Holme enters the river Bure.

Four views of Marsh Farm in April 1984, from Peter Allard Collection.

Ashtree Farm Mill: Left in 1950, from Peter Allard Collection, Right: circa 1960 from Mike Pickard.

ASHTREE FARM DRAINAGE MILL TG507 095

This is shown on the 1996 OS map to south of river in Acle detached parish. Sometimes it is referred to as **Banham's Black Mill**.

The present mill was built in about 1912 by Smithdales of Acle and was owned by the Church Commissioners. It is presently owned by the Banham family and is leased to the Norfolk Windmills Trust, who recently restored the mill as part of 'Land of the Windmills Project'. Millwright Richard Seago did some of the restoration work in 2006 for the Norfolk Windmills Trust. It is a grade 2 listed building. During restoration work in 2005 the tower was jacked upright and new sails were fitted.

The tower brickwork is about 26 ft tall, and to the top of the cap it stands almost 35 feet. It is tarred black and the boat-shaped cap, fantail and petticoat are painted white. The sails are double shuttered patent sails spanning 40 feet. The base of the tower is 14 feet in diameter and the tower has two doors and there are 2 windows on the second floor. The scoopwheel is about 15 feet in diameter and the paddles are 7 inches wide. It could lift about 8 tons of water per minute.

There is striking gear for the sails with rack and pinion and a Y wheel for the striking chain with a tail pole.

It had wooden gear originally and this was replaced in the 1930s with cast iron gear.

On 1st February 1953 it became tail-winded and the sails and windshaft were blown off and the mill was never used again.

An earlier mill was shown here on the 1880s OS map, on the 1838 Tithe map, and was shown as '**Acle Mill**' on Bryant's 1826 map. A mill was marked here on the Acle Enclosure map of 1799 in 'Acle East Marshes' and was owned by Christopher Taylor, but no mill was marked on Faden's 1797 map.

The earlier mill was a cloth sailed mill according to the old millwright A. J. Thrower writing to the EDP 5th Jan 1949.

On the Tithe Map and Apportionment a mill was marked on area 758, listed as 'Mill & Yards'. It was owned by Francis Baas and William Moss was given as the occupier.

On the 1907OS map it was marked as 'Windpump'.

An electric pump was built near to Ashtree Farm in 1949 at about TG503093. This could lift 30 tons per minute.

ASHTREE FARM TG504 093

Ashtree Farm is marked on the 1996 OS map on the south side of river.
This was in the old Acle Detached No 1 Parish.

It was shown on the 1797 map as '**3 MILE HOUSE**' and was marked on the 1799 Acle Enclosure map, as owned by Christopher Taylor. It was also marked on the 1st edition OS map in the 1830s as 'Marsh House'.
It was not marked on the 1826 map!

It was shown on the 1838 Tithe Map at area 753, labelled as 'house and Yards', owned by Frances Baas and occupied by William Moss.

Some occupants at Ashtree Farm, who would have tended the Ashtree Farm Drainage Mill include:

1836 White's directory: William Moss, farmer

1841 census: William Moss, 62, farmer

1861 census: Entry 8: Benjamin Banham, 58, marshman & herdsman. (He was previously at Thurlton)

1901 census: Entry 205: Arthur Palmer, 32, Marsh Labourer, born Billockby.

Arthur Palmer is also listed in the 1916 and 1922 as a farmer.

Later Benjamin Banham, who was listed in 1927 as a cowkeeper in Vauxhall Environs and in 1938 as a farmer at Ferry Farm in Runham Vauxhall, and which is now part of the site of Vauxhall Holiday Park, moved to Ashtree Farm. The Banham family are still here.

3-Mile House from John Lubbock. Harry Smith, the marshman, who lived here built his own boats in one of the sheds here and was a wildfowler on Breydon Water.

THREE MILE HOUSE TG504095

This is in fact a bungalow on the north side of the river inside 'West' Caister parish close to the boundary with Mautby parish.

A dwelling was probably built here in the early 1830s since it was not marked on the 1797 or 1826 maps but was on the 1st edition OS map and on the Tithe map. On the Tithe map it is shown at area 395 and the owner was put as John Edward Lacon and the occupier was Thomas Smith.

The Smith family were here for many years. On the 1891 census at entry 139 'On the Marshes' the occupant was 30 year old marshman Isaac Smith.

Harry Smith was the last marshman here.

It was marked on the 1880s and on the 1996 OS maps.

Harry Smith at 3-Mile House, from John Lubbock.

SCAREGAP PUMP TG49830908

A 'Draining Pump' was marked on 1880s OS map to the south of the river in Acle Detached No 1 parish, near to Scaregap farm. The pump is not shown on the 1907 and later OS maps.

This was not marked on Faden's 1797 map, the Acle Enclosure map, Bryant's 1826 maps nor the 1st edition OS map, but was marked on the Tithe Map of circa 1838 in area 746, 'Cow Marsh', as a '**Steam Engine**'. The owner occupier was listed as Benjamin Heath Baker, who was at Acle Hall. This property was bought in 1830 by Mr Baker from Lancelot Reed. Baker sold the property to William Rivett in 1858. It was later bought by Freeman Eglington in Feb 1878 and then sold to Fleming Hewitt in December of 1878.

The pump is not shown on the circa 1907 and all later OS Maps.

COUNTY COUNCIL COTTAGES

The building shown at TG500089, in the old Acle detached parish, near Scaregap on the 1996 map was built in 1900 next to the Acle New Road. This was a double dweller marked on the 1907 and 1951 OS maps as 'County Council Cottages'. This was originally built to house the workers who looked after the New Road.

SCAREGAP FARM HOUSE TG496089

There was a building here in the Acle Detached parish, which was shown on the 1880s OS map as '**Staregap Farm**' and on the 1951OS maps as '**Scaregap Farm**'. It is not marked on the 1996 map. The buildings here were burnt down in 1972.

Harry Smith, marshman from Three Mile House, showing his catches with his Breydon Water Houseboat in the background. From John Lubbock.

No buildings were shown at this location on the 1797 Faden's map, the Enclosure, Bryant's 1826, or the 1st Edition OS maps, but were shown on the 1838 Acle Tithe Map. These farm buildings were on area 744 which was labelled as House & Garden occupied by William Newson and owned by Benjamin Heath Baker, and area 745 labelled as Buildings and Yards owned and occupied by Benjamin Heath Baker. The buildings must have been erected in the 1830s, probably after the Acle New Road was built. On the earlier Acle Enclosure map of 1799 the land here was owned by George Boult.

The property here was sold in 1858 to Mr William Rivett, then to Freeman Eglinton and then Fleming Hewett. Later owners were Mrs Bessie Holt and Benjamin Charles Sutton.

The early occupants of the dwelling probably operated the nearby Scaregap pump.

Some probable occupants here include:

1841 Acle census: William Newson, 46, Bailiff.

1861 census: entry 9, Rivetts Marsh House: Robert Rushmer, 50, marshman.

1871 census: entry 10, New Rd Near Steam Mill: Robert Rushmer, 60, and William Rushmer, 29, herdsmen.

1881 census entries 8 & 9: William Rushmer, 39 marshman, and Robert Rushmer, 70, farmer.

1891 census: entry 209 Acle Marshes: William Howell, 53, marshfarmer.

1901 census: entry 199 New Road: Willam Howell, 63.

In 1913 Mr S. Howell was living here listed as a Farmer and Dairyman.

Mr Addison lived here for a time.

Harry Smith and his puntgun, from John Lubbock. Harry Smith was one of the last wildfowlers on Breydon Water. He was an excellent shot and had been a sniper in WWI.

Mr Walter Hewitt was the marshman living here in 1960s having moved here from 5 Mile House.

Scaregap Farm from Peter Allard Collection. Top: May 1972 and bottom: ruins in April 1986.

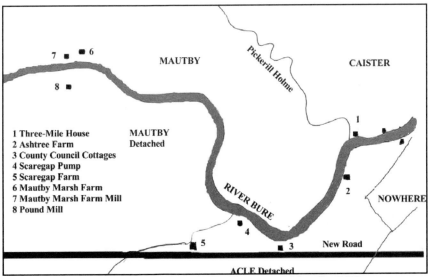

Sketchmap of river between Three-Mile House and Mautby Mills.

MAUTBY SWIM TG490099

A Foot Ferry is shown on the 1826 Bryant's Map and a Ferry is marked on 1880s OS map. Here the cattle were swam across the river.

MAUTBY MARSH FARM TG490099

This is on north side of river in Mautby parish and is shown on the 1996 OS map. This was shown as **FOUR MILE HOUSE** on Faden's map of 1797.

It was not shown on Bryants map but was marked on the 1st edition OS map, on the 1880s OS map and on the Mautby Tithe map. On the Tithe Map it belonged to Robert Fellowes, the Lord of the Manor, at that time.

The occupants here would have worked the nearby Mautby Marsh drainage mill. These include:

1836 White's: Thomas Carpenter, Marsh House.

1841 census: Mautby Mill: Thomas Carpenter, 55, marshfarmer
and David Hewitt, 50, marshman.

1845 Kellys: David Hewitt at Marsh Farm.

1851 census: entry 84 Mautby Swim: David Hewitt, 63, Marsh farmer.

1854 & 1864 Whites: David Hewitt, Marsh Farm

1861 census: entry 5 River Wall: David Hewitt, 73, marshfarmer, and Robert Lawn, 32, marshman: and entry 6 River Wall: Thomas Hewitt, 31, marshman.

1871 census: entry 9 Marsh Farm. Thomas Hewitt, 42, Marshfarmer born Mautby.

1881 census: Thomas Hewitt, 51, Farmer 100 acres, Marsh Farm.

Mautby Mill in 1907 with old steam pump building on the far left and Mautby Marsh Farm buildings on the right with a passing wherry. Peter Allard Collection.

Mautby Mill. Top: circa 1960 from Mike Pickard and bottom: circa 1987 A.C. Smith.

1883 Kellys: Mrs Hewitt, Marsh Farm.

1891 census: entry 19 Swim Farm: James Banham, 29, Marshman born Wickhampton.

1896 Kellys: James Banham, farmer at Marsh Farm.

1901 census: entry 88 Marsh Farm. Fred W. Smith, 30, farmer

Some later marshmen here include:

John Lubbock, who had previously run the Stracey Arms pub, became the marshman here in 1907 and was here till 1931.

John Lubbock jnr. took over and was marshman till 1945.

1937 Kellys: John Lubbock, Marshman

Sidney Nichols was marshman for a short time and the last full time marshman was Bob Newnham who was listed here in 1957 as a farmer and was here till the mid 1960s.

After the house was no longer required for the marshman it was sold as a private dwelling. A Mr Ulph was the first occupant, then a Mr Clarke and then a Mr Andrews, a builder.

MAUTBY MARSH DRAINAGE MILL TG48950995

This is marked on the 1996 OS Map on north side of river in Mautby parish. It is a grade 2 listed building which has been converted into a residence.

This was shown as 'Drain Windmill' on the 1797 map, as '**Mautby Mill**' on the 1826 map, and as a 'draining pump' on the 1880s OS map.

A mill was also marked here on the 1840 Mautby Tithe map on area 189, labelled as 'Mill & Yard', with a house on area 187. The owner was listed as Robert Fellows, the Lord of the Manor, and the occupant of the mill and house was Thomas Carpenter.

The Mautby Estate was sold in 1915 to Lacons Brewery who then became the owners of the Estate and the mill, as the new Lord of the Manor

The first mill here is said to have been built here in 1757.

The present redbrick tower mill is believed to be the third mill built on, or near, this site, and was built about 1903 by Smithdale & Sons. It is said it was built on timber piles driven to a depth of 20 ft. and was capable of lifting 16 tons of water a minute.

The batter of the tower alters at the top suggesting it may have been 'hained' and the tower is three storeys high. It once drove an external scoopwheel. It is believed the windmill was struck by lightening sometime around 1930 and was not used afterwards, the tower being left to become derelict.

The derelict mill was bought in 1981 by Mr Collins and converted into a residential dwelling. John Lawn did some work on the mill. An extension was built onto the mill in about 1986. Mr and Mrs Fenton bought the mill in 1994 and used it as a holiday let charging £250 to £400 during the high season. In July 2002 the mill was put up for sale with a river frontage of 265 feet; with an asking price of £295,000.

The walls of the tower at the base are 3 ft 3ins thick. The renovated mill has a white boat shaped cap with petticoat, gallery and an eight bladed fantail. It has steel stocks and four patent sails without any shutters. The sails are locked in a fixed position. The old stocks from the derelict mill were used during restoration for making the floorboards.

John Lubbock Senior in 1945 from his grandson John Lubbock. He had been licensee at the Stracey Arms before becoming marshman at Mautby Marsh Farm.

A steam turbine was also working here for a few years, and in 1919 a Ruston & Hornsby hot bulb paraffin engine was installed with a 2.5 hp petrol engine for start-up. This could pump up to 30 tons a minute and cost about £2,600. The engine was installed by Thomas Smithdale & Sons in a shed next to the mill. This engine was used till the 1960s and was eventually bought and restored by Mr Bob Morse and went on display in Fleggburgh Village Experience till the museum closed in 2004.

A new pump house was installed a few yards to the west of the old mill in the late 1970s. This has two Archimedes Screw type pumps which together can pump 80 tonnes of water a minute. The new pumps cost about £206,000 with the work that was done to alter and deepen the drains and dykes. This now drains about 990ha of the Caister, Mautby and Runham levels on the north side of the river.

POUND MILL TG489098

This is shown here on the 1826 map in the detached part of Mautby parish on the south side of the river. The 1996 map does not indicate anything here.
The earlier 1797 map indicates two 'Drain W. Mills' near here.

In the Norfolk Chronicle of 15th March 1783 the following is found which may refer to the mills near this location, or to the Mautby mill across the river: ' *To be sold. At Mawtby, in Norfolk, A Skeleton Engine, which works by Wind, and is able to work two pumps that will drain off thirty or forty Acres of Marsh Land; it is in good repair. Enquire of Mr Edmund Woodcock, Millwright at Yarmouth.* '

The Lubbock family in 1946: mother Irene, father John jnr, Grandmother Florence, uncle Alfred Front: brother Gilbert, unknown, John, sister Betty and brother Terry

The 1880s OS map indicates a 'Draining Pump' here and the 1913 map indicates a windmill. The mill had common sails and could lift 10 tons per minute. It was struck by lightning in 1923. Rex Wailes called this mill **RUNHAM LOWER 4 MILE MILL** and said it was a common sail tower mill hained sometime before 1914 and reports that the millwright was Smithdale.

In about 1914 a paraffin engine was installed here and worked till the 1940s when the mill and pump became obsolete when the level was connected to the adjacent level.
The mill here was probably worked by the marshman from the north side of the river at Mautby Marsh Farm. John Lubbock jnr. certainly worked the paraffin engine for Benjamin Sutton in the early 1940s. Arthur Bailey took over here after Lubbock.

58

JOHN LUBBOCK REMEMBERS.

My grandfather, John Lubbock senior, moved into Marsh Farm, Mautby, around 1907. He moved from being the landlord of the Stracey Arms public house on Acle New Road. Grandfather was hard working and enjoyed a glass of beer and was quite a colourful character.

Mautby mill engine at the Fleggburgh Village Experience.
Peter Allard Collection.

The house had 4 bedrooms and a long landing upstairs, 3 living rooms downstairs and a large pantry, and a cellar. Outside the front door there was a well.

John Lubbock junior, my father, took over Marsh Farm around 1930 when grandfather retired. His main work was looking after the oil fired mill, drawing dykes and drains, thistle mowing the marshes, and looking after cattle for a number of owners such as Ben and Maurice Sutton, Harry and Charles Wharton, Oliver Wright and Fred Key etc.

I and my two brothers and one sister were born in the early 1930s and attended Runham School which involved a 4 mile walk, including 1.5 miles over the marshes on unmade road which was a mud-bath in winter with cattle up and down it.

In early 1941 the Bure froze and father and friends skated for 2 or 3 miles and we played football on the ice. The freeze and snow went on for weeks with no let up. The Bure was frozen up to Acle.

During the winter of 1940-41 heavy snow and frosts blocked roads up to 7 feet deep and all we had to eat were biscuits and a few vegetables for 6 days. Marsh farm had no electric, gas or drinking water. The drinking water had to be fetched from Decoy Farm one and a half miles distant.

John Lubbock jnr. (right) working on the marshes near Ashtree farm for the Banham family. From John Lubbock.

During the war an Ack-Ack Gun sight was established on Decoy Farm land and father and mother entertained many of the ATS girls and servicemen from the camp, and father's rowing boat was in constant use by them with trips on the Bure. Shooting parties with the Camps commander, officers and farmers often took place from Marsh Farm as the marshes had plenty of rabbits and wildfowl etc. One item which made news was that the gunners shot down a British Mosquito by mistake and the pilot who baled out came and congratulated them on their shooting.

During the winter months the mill would be used sometimes 24 hours a day, clearing water from the marshes and someone would have to be on hand all the time it was going. 300 gallons of paraffin a time would be delivered by boat from Yarmouth at regular intervals to keep the engine running. An electric mill was installed after the war which needed no regular maintenance and the old mill was made redundant. With the marshes being ploughed up for arable land the living became less and we moved from Marsh Farm towards the end of the war. The marshman's job was dying.

At Three-Mile House down the river Bure Harry Smith was the marshman, a well-known character, being one of the last men using a punt gun on Breydon Water. Harry was a crack shot having been a sniper in the First World War and he could turn his hand to anything, building his own punt and speedboat, he also stuffed birds and animals and had a huge collection which took up a whole room. After his death the collection was sold at Sotherbys in London. Harry and my father were friends and went drinking together on occasions which did not go down too well with his wife and my mother if they had drunk too much!

I look back on these days as happy ones, although being hard we always had friends and relations round and at Christmas the home was always full with the family.

The pleasure steamers Queen of the Broads and Pride of the Yare were up and down the Bure in the summer months and as children we were always on the lookout as passengers would throw sweets to us in passing.

During the war one day there was an early morning raid by Focke Wulf aircraft when my father was working on the marsh with a colleague. They were machine gunned along with a farmer, cattle and horses. Father was not hurt but many cattle were killed and the farmer received a bullet in the leg and his horse was badly injured and had to be put down. Father had a cigarette lighter made from one of the canon shell cases.

Some extracts from my fathers diary:

March 1940: "Met B. Sutton about mill and level over river. Got job.
Started milling over river this afternoon. Took Howells old level as Carter was flooded out. Mill broke"

"Wednesday 5th Feb 1941 Yarmouth had biggest air raid of war about 60 bombs fell in town. Regal Theatre got 100 lb bomb right through roof & exploded in front of stage about half past nine at night. No one killed, a few injured. Some killed in other parts of town."

Draniage Boards Bill for quarter
from July 1st to Sept 30th 1941

Paraffin used during quarter 360 galls

	£	s	d
Running drainage pump 17 days at 8/ day	6	16	0
Drawing 36 score mill dyke at 6/ per score	10	16	0
Drawing 20½ score canal land spring at 7/ per score	7	3	6
Cost of 3 gallons of petrol for engine		5	6
Quarters supervising money	2	10	0
Total	27	11	0

"I rode my bike up canal dyke on ice Sunday March 8th 1942. Ice bound everywhere. Has froze for the last 8 weeks."

"Flywheel bearing seized up on big engine Oct 29th 1942. Smithdale came & got going evening Oct 30th. Mill broke down again Nov 8th – liner ring blew & filled engine with water. Smithdale came Nov 9th. Smithdale finished Mill Monday Nov 16th 1942."

Muckfleet & South Flegg Drainage Board
Dr. To J. Lubbock Marshman Mautby
Marsh Bill for Quarter. Jan 1st to March 31st 1943
(Total oil used in quarter 180 0 galls)

	£	s	d
Running drainage pump decarbineseing engine etc: 85½ days at 10/ per day	42	15	0
Drawing 8½ score cannal land spring at 8/ per score	3	8	0
Drawing 14 score river wall sock dyke at 7/ per score	4	18	0
Drawing 15 score land spring sock dykes at 5/ per score	6	0	0
Cost of 4 galls petrol at 1/11d per gall also one stone rags to clean engine at 5/ stone		12	8
One quarters superviseing money	3	10	0
Total	61	3	8

Bill For Drainage Board May 1943
Btm frying Dyke part Meadows & Flubbins
end

	£	s	d
Bottomfrying 10 chains of landspring dyke near Hall Farm at 28/ chain	14	0	0
Total	14	0	0

Mr: A. Dixon Filby Dr: To J. Lubbock
June 1943

	£	s	d
Btm - frying 12 chains dykes Part 66 etc: at 26/ per chain	15	13	0
Total	15	13	0

63

FIVE MILE HOUSE MILL TG478098

Five Mile House Mill is shown on the 1996 OS map on the south side of the river in the old detached Runham parish. This is a grade 2 listed building protected by the Broads Authority and the Norfolk Windmills Trust.

5mile house circa 1960 from Mike Pickard.

In 2005 the mill was described as a tarred brick tower four storeys high and covered with a temporary aluminium cap. The aluminium cap was put on in 1988. The tower stands about 42 ft to the curb. No floors are present, there is rot in beams and there are cracks over entrance door.

Inside there is a Cast iron windshaft, brake wheel, wallower and crown wheel, Timber upright shaft, Pit wheel and a drive shaft which went to an external scoopwheel.

The pump house is redbrick and the pump is not present.

There was a tablet over a door with WHW 1849 inscribed on it, and on the door of the scoop wheel there was inscribed R.J. Stolworthy 1849. A mill stood here before that date however. A 'Drain W Mill' was marked here on the 1797 map, and **'Runham Mill'** was marked here on the 1826 map. The mill at that time would have driven a scoopwheel and may have had cloth sails.

No mill was shown on the 1st edition OS map, but a mill is shown on the Tithe map circa 1839. On the Tithe map the mill was on area 317 owned by Lady Ann Horne, Henry William Wyre and Rev William Barber. The nearby house on area 310 was occupied by Isaac Gown.

The 1880s OS map shows 'Draining Pump'

An Electric Pump House was built nearby in 1944 and could lift 40 tons per minute.

ARNOLD HEWITT REMEMBERS.

Father Walter Edwin Hewitt moved to Five Mile House in 1928. The house was thatched with three bedrooms. The living room was believed to have been a bar in earlier days where ale was sold to passing wherrymen. There was also a cellar.

The biggest thing I can remember is during the war when a German Bomber dropped a bomb less than ¼ mile from the house on a moonlight night and standing at the corner of the house and watching the plane climb higher. I also remember a line of fire bombs across the marshes stretching from the river to the Acle New Road.

Father moved to Scaregap Farm in about 1960.

Albert Hewitt and Percy Hewitt outside 5 mile house in the early 1930s, from Arnold Hewitt.

POSTWICK DETACHED MARSH HOUSE TG473089

A thatched building was located here on the north side of the Acle New Road in the old detached parish of Postwick, also known as Fuleholme. A building was shown here on the 1880s OS map, but none was shown on Bryant's map.

Henry Bailey lived here and he worked the 5-mile mill on the Bure at one time. In the 1901 Postwick census Henry Bailey was listed as age 46, born Halvergate, listed as a Dairyman. The Bailey family also tended the Runham South Swim Mill for a time.

The building here was destroyed by fire.

RUNHAM SWIM TG475099

A foot ferry was marked here on Bryant's 1826 Map and a ferry on the 1884 OS map.

Local Runham farmer John Howes is said to have 'swam' his cattle across the river here for milking. The bottom of the river here was lined with gravel.

FIVE MILE HOUSE TG475099

FIVE MILE HOUSE on the south side of the river, in the detached Runham Parish, was marked on Faden's map and all later maps. It was built in 1668 and had tie irons in the later days to keep it from falling down.

On Bryant's map it was referred to as '**5 Mile or Swine House**'. It is possible that 'Swine House' should have been 'Swim House' as it was referred to as Swim House in the 1851 census.

On the 1839 Tithe map the house was marked at area 310 and occupant was Isaac Gown. The owners were Lady Ann Horne, Henry William Wyre and Rev William Barber. The occupants of the house probably looked after Five Mile House Mill and perhaps the nearby Runham Swim Mill and also the ferry crossing. *The house is also said to have been a riverside public house called The Swan at one time but no evidence of this is found in the census returns or the trade directories.*

Census and Directory information:

1841 census: Runham Swim: Isaac Gowen, 66, marshman.

1845 Kellys: Isaac Gowen was listed as the Ferryman.

1851 census: entry 11 Swim House: Charles Gowen, 39 marsh farmer 123 acres.

1861 census: entry 65: Charles Gowen, 49, marshfarmer.

1869 & 1875 Kellys list Robert Thaxter as a farmer and Ferryman.

1871 census: entry 70 Swim House. Robert Thaxter, 50, Marshfarmer.

1881: Possibly William Dyble, 68, Marsh labourer.

1883 Whites: John Palmer, farmer & ferryman.

1891: John Palmer, 35, marshman.

1896: John Palmer, cowkeeper & marshman, Runham Swim.

1901: John Palmer, 46, marshman, bn Runham.

1908: J. Palmer, Marshman, Runham Swim.

1916: John Palmer Cowkeeper, Runham Swim.

1925: John Palmer Cowkeeper, Runham Swim.

Walter Hewitt was the cowkeeper / marshman at Runham Swim from 1928 until the late 1950s before moving to Scaregap Farm.

Five Mile House Drainage Mill in 1987 from AC Smith.

Five-Mile Drainage Mill. Peter Allard Collection. Left: as when in working order. Right: 4th April 1969.

Old chicken shed made from old windmill vanes not far from 5-Mile House in the mid 1960s. Supplied by Mike Pickard

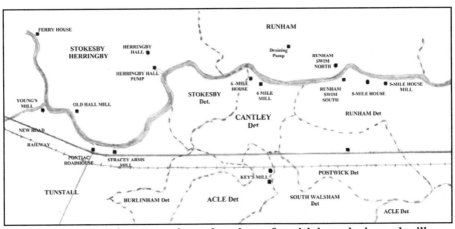

Sketch map illustrating approximate locations of parish boundaries and mills.

**Runham Swim South Mill, often known as Perry's Mill, in working order.
Peter Allard Collection.**

RUNHAM SWIM SOUTH DRAINAGE MILL TG472099

This is shown on the 1996 OS map to the south of the river as **RUNHAM SWIM DRAINAGE MILL**.

It is often called '**PERRY'S MILL**' and is a grade 2 listed building looked after by the Norfolk Windmill Trust. It is a tarred redbrick tower of 3 storeys about 28 ft high, with an aluminium cap and much of the internal machinery survives. It drove an external turbine pump.

It was marked on the 1884 OS map as a 'draining pump' and all later maps, but was **not** shown on the Tithe Map circa 1840, nor on the earlier Bryant's 1826 and Faden's1797 Maps.

David Childs remembers that the Bailey family who lived on Acle New Road worked this mill at one time.

RUNHAM SWIM NORTH DRAINAGE MILL TG471100

This is marked on the north side of the river on the 1996 OS map as **RUNHAM DRAINAGE MILL**. This was shown on the 1884 OS map as a 'drainage pump' and a mill was marked on Bryant's map but NOT on the 1797 Faden's map.

On the Tithe Map and Apportionment of 1839 the mill was located on area 243 and the mill house on area 242. The owner occupier was listed as the 'Commissioners of Drainage'.

In 1841 census Benjamin Howes, age 45, marshman was listed at Marsh Mill.

1851 census: Mill House: William Howes, 31.

1861 census: River Wall: William Howes, 43.

1881 census: Marshes: William Howes, 63, marshfarmer and Robert Lawn, 52.

1891 census: Entry 27 Swim Road: John Howes, 52 marshman.

1901 census: Mill: Robert Lawn, 74, marshman, and Charles Lawn 26, marshman.

This mill is often called **CHILDS MILL** as the last occupants at the mill house were the Childs family. William Lawn 'Hawke' Childs was here from about 1917 to 1951.

Mr Watt bought the mill and millhouse in the mid 1950s for about £30.

The mill is now leased to Norfolk Windmills Trust and is a grade 2 listed building.

The mill was a tarred redbrick tower 3 storeys high, about 30 ft to the curb with a white boat-shaped cap and petticoat. The mill had an internal scoopwheel and stopped working in about 1937. It had an 8 bladed fantail. It has 2 doors and 1 window. Rex Wailes called this **RUNHAM COMMISSION MILL** and said 'the internal scoopwheel had an internal spur ring cast on the scoop wheel spider for drive by a Tangue hot bulb oil engine with one spur reduction between it and the crankshaft; this was in addition to the bevel ring cast on for the wind drive.' Wailes says it was built in 1819 by a Midland Firm.

Some restoration work was started in 1983, and Richard Seago did some work on this mill.

Runham Swim North Mill in 1930 from David Childs (George Havis from Smithdales of Acle is at the top of sails).

Runham Swim North mill house when the Childs family lived here (David Childs).

Runham Swim North Mill in April 1956 before the mill house was to be demolished, looking towards the north east, from Peter Allard Collection.

William Childs and Walter Palmer cleaning dykes on Runham marshes in 1932, supplied by David Childs.

Left: Millwrights from Englands working on the Runham Mill. Right: William Childs and son David by the Runham mill, supplied by David Childs.

William Childs by the Runham Mill in 1918, supplied by David Childs.

Runham Swim North mill in working order. The mill in the distance is the South Runham Swim Mill. From David Childs.

Runham Swim North Mill circa 1960 M. Pickard.

DAVID CHILDS REMEMBERS.

My father, William Lawn Childs, moved to Runham Swim in 1917 and was the marshman here till he died in 1951. We were allowed to continue to live at the mill house till 1953. I worked for some years for Smithdales, the Acle millwrights and visited many of the pumps and mills along the river.

We had no electric at the millhouse and father used to bike to Mr Hunt's in Filby to have the accumulators recharged for the wireless. Paraffin was used for lighting and a well was sunk in the 1940s.

In 1953 the marshes around the mill house were flooded but we had no water come into the house.

The sails on the Runham North mill were very long and only cleared the floor by about one foot. The sails were removed in 1939. There was the remains of the footings

75

of an earlier building here which may have been an earlier steam pump house.

Robin Harrisson hired the cottage next to Dack's Mill.

Steve and John Lock, from the mill house at Stokesby Commission Mill used to catch eels near Acle Bridge, on the Yarmouth side. Later in the 1950s Arthur Rice used to catch eels here. They used to put a net across the river and have a post and winch on either side. This was usually done at night when there was no river traffic. The catch was put in a water-filled tank till the catch was big enough to put on the train at Acle Station.

Kerrison's Mill with the mill house in the right background.
Peter Allard Collection.

KEY'S MILL TG462085

Sometimes called '**Black Mill**' or '**Kerrison's Mill**', lying on Kerrison's Level, this mill lies some distance from the river and on the south side of the Acle New Road and the railway line. It pumped water into a dyke which runs into the Bure. This mill last worked in the mid 1940s and is located in the old Acle Detached Parish. It is a grade 2 listed building and is currently looked after by the Norfolk Windmills Trust and was leased for 99 years to the Norfolk County Council in 1982.

No mill was shown here on the 1797 map or the 1799 Acle Enclosure map, but a mill was shown on Bryant's map and all subsequent maps. Bryant's 1826 map shows this as '**Acle Mill**'

On the Acle Tithe Map of 1838 a mill was marked on area 708 and a house on area 707. The owner and occupier of the house and mill was given as Mathias Harrison.

This is a redbrick tower mill, tarred black, four storeys high and is about 32 ft high to the curb. It has a window on the second floor and another on the top floor. The inside diameter at the base is about 12 ft 9 inches, and the wall thickness is 18 inches. Six metal bands encircle the tower and the barter changes at the top suggesting it was 'hained' at some time. It also has two metal tie-rods. It has a white boat shaped cap with petticoat, but no sails or stocks. The external scoopwheel is about 17 ft 3 inches in diameter.

It was repainted in 1987 and again in 2000.

The mill was attended to for many years by the Bailey family who lived in the nearby farmhouse. From the censuses we find:

1841 census: Richard Kerrison, 25, marshman
1861 census: entry no. 10, 'Kerrison's Marsh House': Samuel Bailey, 51, marshman.
1881 census: entry no. 7: Samuel Bailey, 72, marshman, 30 acres.
1891 census: entry no. 208, Acle Marshes: Frederick Bailey, 30, marshfarmer.
1901 census: entry no. 198, New Road: William Bailey, 22, marshfarmer.
The Kelly's directories for 1916, though to 1937 all list William Henry Bailey as a marshman at Acle. In 1948 Mrs Bailey was given as the marshman (NRO/BR143/114).

In March 1938 the mill, marshman's house and 261 acres of Kerrison's Level was put up for sale. The mill was in working order and drained about 380 acres; the mill rents amounting to £25-15s-6d. The marshman was W. Bailey. (ref NRO/BR143/113).

In 1950 Kerrison's Level was sold again by direction of G.C. Hughes. The level was 260 acres and included the old now disused mill and the marshman's house. The sitting tenant in the house was marshman W. Parker whose annual rent was £10. The house is brick built, and at that time was part tiled and part thatched.

From 1952 the marshman on Kerrison's Level living at 'Black Mill Farm' was W. R. Mallett. The Hon Major H.R. Broughton was the owner of Kerrison's Level in 1960 (NRO/BR143/115).

Kerrison's Mill in working order. Peter Allard Collection.

Top: Billy Mallett and his son Paul on 5th September 1995.
Bottom: The mill house on Kerrison's level on 14th June 1969.
Peter Allard Collection.

Kerrison's Level house being re-thatched, 12th May 1995 by thatcher Derek Rolls. Peter Allard Collection.

A Drainage Pump shown here on the 1884 OS map.
It was not shown on Faden's or Bryant's map and was probably a steam engine pump.
It is not shown on the 1997 OS map.

SIX MILE HOUSE DRAINAGE MILL TG461098

SIX MILE HOUSE DRAINAGE MILL is shown on the 1996 OS map on the south side of the river. It is a grade 2 listed building. This area was once the detached part of Cantley parish.

A mill was marked here on all maps from 1797, and was marked as 'Drain W Mill' on Faden's 1797 map, as **'CANTLEY MILL'** on Bryant's 1826 map, and as a 'draining pump' in 1884. It has been called by several other names including **BLAKE'S MILL** and **LAKE'S MILL** and **WLLIAM PERRY'S MILL**. On the Cantley Tithe Map & Apportionment, circa 1840, area 233 is marked as 'Mill, House & Yards etc' and is owned by Mrs Shuckford and occupied by Isaac Gown jnr.

The present mill is a tarred redbrick tower mill, four storeys high with an external scoopwheel. The tower has a lean and corrugated sheeting is on the top. It is a grade 2 listed building. This last mill is believed to have been built in the 1870s and last worked in the mid 1940s.

The building firm of R.G. Carter owned the mill, house and several acres here at one time and they sold it in about 1976.

It is now privately owned.

There is a pump house nearby.

Smith in 1987 said it had no cap, but had stocks and 2 patent sails and internal machinery.

Some of the marshmen here from the Cantley census returns were:
1851 census: Isaac Gowen, 46 marsh farmer
1861 Isaac Gown, 57, born Langley (at Raven Hall on the Haddiscoe Island)
1871 George Thaxter, 42, marsh farmer, born Reedham (probably related to the Thaxter family at Polkey's Mill, Seven Mile Reedham)
1881 George Thaxter, 52, marshman, bn Reedham
1891 George Thaxter, 60, marshman, bn Reedham
1901 Frederick Bailey, 41. (previously at Kerrison's Mill in Acle detached)
Mr Robert Lake was the marshman in the 1930s and 1940s.

Six-Mile Mill in working order from Brian Grint.

Six Mile Mill, with the scoopwheel exposed, from Brian Grint.

SIX MILE HOUSE TG459099

This is to the south of the river and was marked on the 1797 map, Bryants Map and the 1st OS map of the 1830s. On the tithe Map and Apportionment of circa 1840 the owner was given as Mrs Shuckford and the occupier as Isaac Gown jnr.

The conveyance of freehold hereditaments provides the following early information about the property:
In August 1848 conveyance of property from John & Clement Palmer to Isaac Gowen.
In 1869 Isaac Gowen leased the property to Geoerge Thaxter for 15 years.
In July 1875 the executors of Isaac Gowen auctioned the property and it was purchased by William Parry of Hemsby for £2560.

The house is now owned by Mr Philip Lennard.

David Childs remembers that there was a wide crack in the east wall which was about 6 inch wide at the top. The gable end was shored up in the 1970s.

The house stands on a slightly raised mound. The west gable appears to be 18th century but the south face is believed to be of early 19th century, and the north extension of late 19th century build. Excavations in recent years for installing cables and sewers have revealed sherds of grey pottery and layers of black soot believed to predate 1300. Other finds included straw-impressed clamp fired bricks, and burnt red earth with layers of charcoal. It is believed that the finds may point to an early salt boiling site here and perhaps a later brick making site.

Philip Lennard by the excavations at 6-Mile House which are believed to be part of the remains of a salt works here. Peter Allard Collection.

HERRINGBY HALL PUMP TG447100

A DRAINING PUMP was marked here in the Stokesby & Herringby Parish on the 1884 OS map on the north side of the river a short distance away from Herringby Hall. It was not shown on the 1840 Tithe Map, or on earlier maps. It was marked on the 1950's OS map, but is not shown on the 1996 map.

Originally this was a steam engine drainage pump owned by the Waters family at Herringby Hall. The Waters family were at Herringby Hall for many years, and in 1851 William Waters, age 48, was listed as a farmer of 330 acres at Hall Farm Herringby.

The steam pump was replaced by an electric pump in about 1936 by the Drainage Board with agreement with Charlie Waters, and Herringby Hall had electricity put on at the same time.

A relict Salt Works site was marked on the 1880s OS map near Dove House Farm in Stokesby & Herringby.

STRACEY ARMS MILL TG442090

STRACEY ARMS MILL lies to the south of the river and was in Tunstall parish. This is often called **ARNUP'S MILL** since it was worked by several members of the Arnup family.

A mill was marked here on the 1884 OS map as a 'draining pump'. On the 1826 map a mill was shown here as **TUNSTALL MILL**, and on Faden's map it was marked as 'Drain W Mill'.

On the Tithe Map, circa 1840, a mill was marked on area 147, which was listed as the Mill Marsh. It was owned by Edward Stracey and occupied by Christmas Francis, who was at the Stracey Arms public house according to the Tithe Apportionment. The adjacent building on area 148 was listed as 'Cottage & Garden' and was listed as owned and occupied by Edward Stracey. (Stracey, however, did not live in this building.) This was the dwelling where many of the subsequent marshmen lived.

This mill is now owned by Norfolk County Council and looked after by Norfolk Windmills Trust. It was previously owned by the Stracey family, hence the name, and was gifted to the council by Lady Stracey in 1965.

The mill marked here on the early maps would have been a primitive mill.

The present mill is a red brick tower, three storeys high, and about 36 feet to the top of the tower. The inside diameter at the base is 10 ft 6 in and at the top of the brick work it is 6 ft. 9 inches in diameter. It is said to have been built, or rebuilt, in 1883 by Richard Barnes, of Gt. Yarmouth, on 40 foot piles topped with a raft of pitchpine. At that time it was a patent sail mill and drove a scoopwheel. A turbine pump was installed later by Smithdales of Acle in 1912.

During WWII the mill was used as a pillbox by the home guard.

A 20hp electric pump was built here in about 1942 and took over from the mill. It could lift 28 tons per minute.

Stracey Arms Mill in March 1944, from the Peter Allard Collection.

Smithdales of Acle did some restoration work on the mill in 1961 and more restoration work has continued under the guidance of the Norfolk Windmills Trust. John Lawn did some work on the mill for the Norfolk Windmills Trust.

It now has a white boat-shaped cap and petticoat, gallery, 8-bladed fantail, Y wheel and tailpole. It has patent sails which are no longer able to turn, having been fixed to avoid the pumphouse below being struck. The sails turned clockwise. There is one door, 2 windows on the first floor and 2 windows on the top floor.
The external turbine pump and the machinery inside the mill still exist.

The mill house nearby was where the millman or marshman lived.

Some of the occupants were:

1841: William Arnup, 35 Ag Lab
1851: entry 2: William Arnup, 45 marsh labourer, born Rackheath.
1871: entry 21: William Arnup, 65, marshman
1881: George Arnup, 36, marshman and son George, 16 marshman
1891: entry119: George Arnup, 46, marshman
1901: George Arnup, 55, stockman on marshes.

1896, 1900, 1916 & 1925 Kelly's Directories: George Arnup, marshman.

1937 Kelly's Directory: Leonard Arnup, marshman.

Fred Mutton was marshman here in the 1940s. 50s & 60s.

'Paddy' Walker lived in the mill house in the 1970s and his wife looked after the mill which was open to the public. The mill house incorporates a small shop and offers provisions for boating holiday-makers.

Wherries on the Bure near the Stracey Arms in 2001: Norada, Olive and Harthor at the rear.

This is the first safe moorings for holiday cruisers since the Yarmouth Marina about seven miles down river.

PONTIAC ROADHOUSE TG438090

This was originally the **STRACEY ARMS PUBLIC HOUSE** and lies to the south of the river and adjacent to New Road. It is in the old parish of Tunstall.

The name was altered to **The THREE FEATHERS** in 1999 and it is now called **The PONTIAC ROADHOUSE**.

In October 2007 it was put up for sale with an asking price of oiro £750,000.

A building was marked here on the 1797, 1826 and first edition OS map of 1830's as **'SEVEN MILE HOUSE'**. It is probable that it first became a public house in the 1830s after the New Road was built.

It was marked on the Tithe Map as '**Stracey Arms**' on area 145, the owner was Edward Stracey and the occupier at that time was Christmas Francis.

It has probably been altered and rebuilt several times. The present buildings were built in the 1960s.

BLOFIELD & WALSHAM LICENCE REGISTERS list this as an Alehouse.

Some past owners include: Sir HENRY STRACEY of Rackheath, Sir EDWARD STRACEY of Rackheath, BULLARDS by 1903 and WATNEY MANN on 4th April 1967.

Licensees / Occupants	Comments	Dates
ROBERT CROWE	victualler	1836
CHRISTMAS FRANCIS	Aged 49 in 1851 census	1841
JOSEPH POWLEY		1854
JOHN POWLEY		1856
JAMES WILKINS		1858 - 1861
THOMAS ENGLAND SAMSON		1864
SCURRELL YOUNGS	Aged 33 in 1871 census & a farmer 18 acres. Son James was born here in 1868.	1868
WALTER THURTLE		13.05.1889
HENRY SPENCER RAYNER	Aged 25 in 1891 census	19.01.1891
THOMAS BRINDID		06.07.1891
JOHN ROBERT LUBBOCK		12.11.1900
BENJAMIN EDWARD ALLEN	16.12.1918 - Fine of 5/-, or 7 days detention for allowing consumption out of hours.	18.11.1907
ROBERT MARTIN MALLETT	25.08.1919 - Fine of £3, or 21 days detention for allowing consumption during prohibited hours.	13.01.1919
GEORGE MOLL		17.05.1920

DAVID ALFRED WILLIAM EASTER		14.11.1921
EDWARD JOHN BRUNSON		15.05.1922
HANNAH BRUNSON		04.02.1935
JOHN WILLIAM MUSKETT		24.06.1935
BENJAMIN EDWARD BLAKE		23.03.1953
ALEX BABLOT		09.04.1962
EDWARD KENDLE THACKERAY		29.11.1965
JOHN CYRIL GREEN		13.06.1966
EDWARD KENDLE THACKERAY		06.02.1967
SAMUEL JOSEPH CHAPMAN		25.03.1968
EDWARD KENDLE THACKERAY		06.01.1969
ALAN HULME		24.11.1969
COLIN ERNEST HOWES		31.03.1970
JOHN LEONARD BURCHALL		12.02.1973

The Pontiac Roadhouse in 2008.

OLD HALL DRAINAGE MILL G436095

Old Hall (Dack's) Mill in working order.

OLD HALL DRAINAGE MILL is shown on the east of the river on the 1996 OS map. This has sometimes been called **DACK'S MILL** and was in the Stokesby parish.

Dack's mill cottage circa 1960 from Mike Pickard.

It was shown on Faden's 1979 map as 'Drain W Mill', on Bryant's 1826 map as **'Stokesby Mill'** and as a 'Draining Pump' on the 1884 and 1950 OS maps. On the tithe map of 1839 a cottage is shown at area 332, area 333 is called the Mill Marsh and area 334 is called Mill and Rand. The owner occupier was given as George Copeman, who was Lord of the Manor.

This was a common sailed tarred brick tower mill that drove a scoopwheel.

AC Smith in 1990 described the mill as a privately owned derelict small tarred red brick tower mill that had worked a scoopwheel, with a derelict thatched cottage nearby. Rex Wailes said this mill was winded with a tailpole.

Old Hall Mill in 1980s from AC Smith

TUNSTALL DYKE TG432095

Tunstall Dyke is about 0.8 mile long and runs in a WSW direction from the south side of the river passing under the Acle New Road and the Acle –Yarmouth railway. It was at one time navigable and at the end of the dike is Tunstall Staithe, where the Powley family once lived in a wooden building and kept a trading wherry. The family were also coal dealers.

The last wherry to navigate the dyke is reported to have been 'The Albert and Alexandra' in about 1897. This was an 18 ton wherry owned by Joseph Powley. When unloaded it was difficult to get the vessel under the New Road hump-back Tunstall Bridge and under the railway bridge. It was also difficult to negotiate the bridges when fully laden when the water level was low.

The Powley family had previously owned a wherry called 'Tunstall Trader' and a 14 ton wherry called 'The Maid'.

1891 census: Entry No. 122: Tunstall Boat Dyke: Joseph Powley, 82, wherry owner.
1881 census: Entry Boat House: Joseph Powley, 71, coal merchant
    And Entry Boat House: William Powley, 48, waterman

1871 census: Entry 16: Joseph Powley, 61, boatman, and William Powley, 38, boatman

1861 census: entry 119: William Powley, boatman

1851 census: entry 7: Joseph Powley, 41, boatman,   William Powley, 19, boatman and Joseph Powley, 17, boatman.

1841 census: Joseph Powley, 30, boatman,   And John Powley, 23, boatman.

Top: Young's Mill circa 1938. Bottom: Young's Millhouse.
Peter Allard Collection

Young's Mill in July 1924. From Brian Grint Collection

YOUNGS MILL TG432096

A 'drainage pump' was shown on the south side of the Tunstall Dyke, where the dyke enters the Bure, on the OS maps of circa 1884, 1907 and 1951.

A mill was also shown here on the Tunstall Tithe Map, circa 1840, on the area numbered 137. It was owned and occupied at that time by Isaac Everit. The adjacent area 136, was shown as 'house and yards' and was occupied then by John Howell and owned by Isaac Everit.

John Howell was probably responsible for operating the mill here and was listed in the 1851 census at entry no.6 , as age 53, occupier of 40 acres, and in 1861, entry 120 Marsh House, as age 62, Marshfarmer. Others that may have lived here are:
1871 census: either William Rumbold, 42, marshman or Robert Turner, 66, marshman;
1881 census: Marsh House: William Rumbold, 51, marshman, or Marsh House Cottage: Robert Turner, 76, marshman.
1891 census: entry 121, The Marshes: Scurrell Youngs, 53 marshman.
1896, 1925 directories: Scurrell Youngs, marshfarmer.
1925, 1933, 1937 directories: George Youngs.
George Youngs was still living here as a marshman in the 1940s.

The last mill here was a cloth sailed tower mill believed to have been built in 1818. The mill was shown on Bryant's map of 1826 as '**Tunstall Mill**'.
Faden's Map of 1797 also shows an earlier mill here.
The level here was sometimes referred to as Gowing's Level.

The old mill house was pulled down and a new dwelling has been erected on the site.

An electric PUMPING STATION is shown on the 1996 map where Tunstall Dyke meets the river.

The top spindle of Young's mill 4th April 1969. Peter Allard Collection

TUNSTALL DYKE DRAINAGE MILL TG422092

Marked on the 1826 and all subsequent maps it lies on the north side if the dyke in the parish of Tunstall. No mill was marked here on the 1797 map.

On the Tithe Map this was area 59 marked as 'Mill & Yard', owned by Stephen Bailey and occupied by James Skinner.

A mill is marked here on the 1996 OS Map as '**Tunstall Dyke Drainage Mill**'. This is a grade 2 listed building and was a 4 storey brick tower mill and had an external scoopwheel of 13 ft 4 inch diameter. The tower is about 24 ft to the curb and the external diameter at the base is about 16ft. Walls are 2 ft thick at the base of the tower. There are 2 doors and a ground floor window, 2 windows on the first floor and a further window at second floor level.

A. C. Smith writing in 1990 said that it was in a very derelict state but had an iron rack on top and an iron pit wheel of 7 ft diameter, its shaft going to the external scoop wheel.

1841 census James Skinner, 50 farmer.
1851 census James Skinner, 34 farmer of 163 acres.
James Skinner was also listed in the 1854 and 1864 directories as a farmer.

Tunstall Dyke Tower Mill July 1988 from AC Smith.

TUNSTALL SMOCK DRAINAGE MILL TG423092

This is marked on the 1996 OS map. This was also shown on the 1951 OS map and the 1907 OS map as a 'drainage pump'. This is in the parish of Tunstall and is located on the south east side of Tunstall Dyke.

On the OS map of circa 1884 the mill was **not** shown here but another 'drainage pump' was shown closer to the Tunstall Staithe at about TG421091.

On the earlier Tunstall Tithe Map and on Bryant's map of 1826 a mill was again marked at TG423092. A 'Drain W Mill' was also marked near here on Faden's map of 1797, but the exact location is not clear.

On the Tithe Map area 91 was marked as 'Mill & Yard', the owner was Andrew Fountaine and the occupier listed as Richard Gillett. Richard Gillett is also listed in 1851 census as farmer, age 63, of 270 acres. He was also listed in the 1854 directory as a farmer.

The early mill at TG 423092 must have become obsolete and another 'pump' was built at TG421091 near the staithe sometime before the 1880s, and then a further mill was built on, or near, the original site around the turn of the century.

According to AC Smith writing in 1989 the smock mill here was derelict and was reduced to about 12 ft in height. It was octagonal in shape with horizontal boards and had a boarded shed attached. He says it contained no machinery at that time, but had once had an internal turbine pump.

It is truncated to 2 storeys and about 2/3rds of its original height and was given a sloping corrugated iron roof in 1994.

Tunstall Dyke Smock Mill in 1989 May from AC Smith.

In about 1941 an electric pump was installed nearby and this could pump up to 25 tons of water per minute.

Some marshmen listed in the parish of Tunstall that may have operated these Tunstall mills include:
1871 census: William Rumbold, 42 or Robert Turner, 66;
1881 census: Marsh House: William Rumbold, 51, or Marsh House Cottage: Robert Turner, 76.
1891 census: Halvergate Road: Edward Youngs, 28.

FERRY HOUSE TG431105.

This public house is next to the river and on The Green in Stokesby. The present building was built in 1890. It has also been called the **FERRY BOAT INN** and the **FERRY INN**.
EAST & WEST FLEGG LICENCE REGISTERS list this as an Alehouse and gives some of the owners as LACONS, WHITBREAD, and ADNAMS.

Occupant / licensee	Comments / Notes	Date
JOHN ROWLAND	Age 50 in 1841	1836 - 1845
EDWARD SAUL	age 58 in 1851	1851 - 1854
JOHN BROWNE		1856 - 1858
WILLIAM SOUTHGATE	& farmer	1861 - 1877
ELIJAH THURTLE	1891 vict & farmer. Age 69 in 1901, lic. Vict. Born Horning	C1879
MARIA THURTLE		10.02.1903
JOHN WILLIAM PALMER		12.01.1904
EDGAR ROBERT ALLEN		08.01.1907
WILLIAM GEORGE LINFORD		03.11.1914
HERBERT PRESTON	Fine 20/- or 14 days detention for selling out of hours 28.07.1925	04.01.1921
RICHARD DRIVER		25.04.1933
HAROLD DAVEY NEWBY		29.10.1940
ETHEL IRENE NEWBY		04.02.1941
HAROLD DAVEY NEWBY		16.07.1946
TRACY T. BEAN		Currently

STOKESBY FERRY TG431105
This is marked on all the old maps adjacent to the public house but became defunct after the 'New Road' from Stokesby to the A1064 was constructed.

STOKESBY VILLAGE

Although the parish of Stokesby cum Herringby is quite extensive and has detached portions on the south of the River Bure, the village itself lies close to the river. In past times the village had a blacksmiths, a post office, public houses, various shops and a corn windmill.

The old post office is today the Candle Centre.

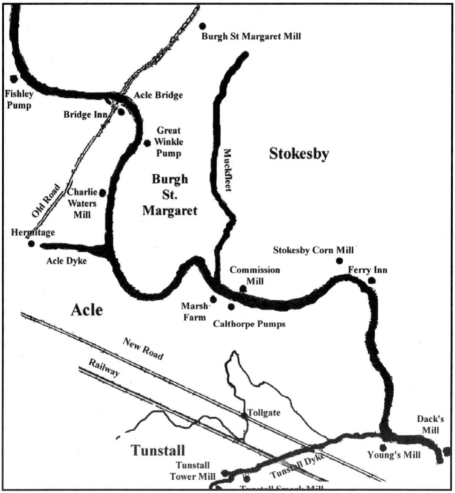

Map from Dack's (Old Hall) Mill to Fishley Mill with parishes and mills marked.

Top: Gowen Series postcard circa 1930 showing the riverside upstream from the Stokesby Ferry Inn.
Bottom: The Stokesby Riverside Tea Rooms in 2008.

Postcard view of the Stokesby Ferry Inn circa 1914.

Stokesby Ferry Inn in 2008.

STOKESBY CORNMILL TG42951067

Stokesby cum Herringby towermill was a 5 storey, tarred red brick mill. It was not marked on Faden's or Bryant's maps, so was probably built after 1826.
It drove 2 pairs of stones.
In 1888 an Auxiliary steam power engine was installed.
It was last worked by Edward Elijah Trett jnr. who was renting the mill from his father, Edward Elijah Trett snr. When Edward snr. died in 1916 the mill was put up for auction and probably never worked again.

Postcard view of Stokesby Corn Windmill in working order.

Stokesby Millers from census returns, newspaper cuttings, and trade directories include the following:

The Norfolk Chronicle of 19th December 1829: *'Stokesby Mill to be sold or let. All that well built brick Tower Wind Mill with patent sails and winding tackle complete, brick and tilled dwelling house, granary, stable, outbuildings, garden and about one acre of excellent arable land situate in the centre of the parish of Stokesby in the county of Norfolk, within 7 miles of Gt. Yarmouth and only a few yards distant from a good staithe, adjoining a fine river where numerous Keels and Wherries are passing daily. The premises stand exceedingly well for an extensive trade, are in the best possible state of repair, being newly erected upon the best and most improved plans and the mill drives 2 pair of stones, flour mill, jumper etc. with plenty of room in the tower for any further addition. Apply to Mr Robert Porter of Martham or to Mr James Page on the premises.'*

White's 1836: Robert Ransome, corn miller.

The Tithe Map & Apportionment circa 1840: Robert Ransome is listed as owner & occupier of area 195 'House, Mill, Yard & Gardens'.

1841 census: Robert Ransome, 55, miller at Mill House.

White's 1845: Robert Ransome, miller.

Census 1851: The Mill: John P. Bartram (23) bn. Filby, miller employing 1 man.

1853: John Durrant.

White's 1854: George Durrant, corn miller.

1858: George Greenacre.

Put up for sale 28th July 1860.

White's 1864: Thomas Capon, corn miller.

Census 1871: Thomas Capon, miller.

1874: Edward Mayhew.

2nd October 1878 Put up for sale.

Kelly's 1879: James Frosdick, miller & shopkeeper.

Census 1881: James Frosdick (34) bn. Stokesby, miller & grocer.

White's 1883: James Frosdick, miller, shopkeeper, pork butcher and overseer.

3rd August 1889 Yarmouth Independent: *'On Tuesday next at 12 o'clock Immediate sale. James Woolterton will sell by auction under an execution from the Sheriff of Norfolk upon the premises in the occupation of Mr James Frosdick. A nearly new powerful 7HP portable engine and boiler by Holmes and Sons of Norwich'*

The mill, dwelling houses, blacksmith's shop and over 4 acres of land was sold at the Star Hotel by auction on 12 March 1890. Edward Elijah Trett of Filby bought the mill.

Census 1891: Edward E. Trett (21) bn. Filby, miller & corn chandler.

Kelly's 1896: Edward E. Trett, miller (steam & wind)

Census 1901: Edward E. Trett, 31 miller & corn merchant.

1916: Edward Elijah Trett jnr.

On the 19th May 1917 the Yarmouth Independent had the following: *'Stokesby Mill with house & land for sale by auction by Spelmans on instructions from the Executors of E. E. Trett, decd. will sell by Auction on 6 June 1917 at the Star Hotel, Great Yarmouth'.*

Mr Edward Youngs was the owner of the derelict mill at one time.

The cap was removed in the 1970s but the mill was weatherproof and still contained some machinery. The tower has been truncated and it has been roofed.

Stokesby corn mill tower in 2008.

COMMISSION DRAINAGE MILL TG422104

This is marked with this name on the 1996 OS map on the north side of the river in Stokesby parish. A windmill was shown here on the Stokesby map of 1721 (NRO/MC351/2) and was owned by the then Lord of the Manor, George England. A mill was also marked here on the 1797 map as '**Stokesby Drain Mill**', on the 1826 map as '**Stokesby Mill**', and on the 1880s OS map and the 1950s OS map as a 'drainage pump'. A mill was also shown on the 1830s 1st Edition OS map and on the Tithe Map.

On the Stokesby Tithe Map, circa 1840, area 149 is listed as 'House, Garden & Mill' and was owned and occupied by Knights Francis Daniel.

The early mills here would have been very primitive mills and the last mill erected here probably dates from the mid to late nineteenth century. It is believed to have been built by Rust of Martham. This was a redbrick tower mill which drove a scoopwheel and is now privately owned and converted with a flat roof. Rex Wailes said 'the cast iron mortice pit wheel had spur teeth on the rim which took an auxiliary drive from an ancient vertical steam engine by Smithdale of Acle.'

The nearby mill-cottage is thatched.

Some Marshmen listed at Stokesby that may have been responsible for operating this or other mills in Stokesby include:
1851 census entry 60 Benjamin Miller, 37 Ag Lab.
1871 census entry 91: Benjamin Miller, 56, Marshman.
1875 James Golder listed as farmer.
1881 census: James Golder, 49, Marsh Farmer, bn. Stokesby and Charles Rumbold, 38, marshman, bn Acle.
1891 census: Water Mill House: Charles Rumbold, 48, farmer.
1901 census entry 1 Riverside: Charles Rumbold, 58, farmer.
1908 & 1922 Charles Rumbold, farmer at Manor Farm.
1933 & 37: James Debbage, marshman.
David Childs recalls that the Lock family lived in the millhouse here and were followed by Horry Tooley.

Stokesby Commission Mill.
Top: circa 1930 from an Osborne Series postcard.
Bottom circa 1985 from AC Smith.

On the south side of the river in the parish of Acle on Calthorpe Level Marshes, and almost opposite the Stokesby Commission Drainage Mill there was two '**drainage pumps**' marked on the circa 1884 OS map. These were only a few meters apart and both marked to the east of Marsh Farm, which is located at about TG 421103.

Acle Calthorpe Level marsh farm mills with Stokesby Commission Mill on the right.

The later 1907 and 1950's OS maps show the pump at the east now as a '**disused draining pump**', but the other pump to the west was still marked as a '**draining pump**' indicating it was still in use.

Faden's 1797 map had a mill at about this location marked as '**Acle Drain W Mill**'. Bryant's map of 1826, however, does not show a mill here, but instead shows a mill, marked as '**Acle Mill**', just to the *west* of the location of Marsh Farm, so assuming the map is correct this suggests the early mill on Faden's map had been replaced sometime between 1797 and 1826. The 1830s 1st Edition OS map and the 1838 Tithe map once again show one mill located to the east of the location of Marsh Farm possibly suggesting another mill rebuild sometime after 1826.

(The 1ˢᵗ Edition Os map does not mark Marsh Farm itself, but only shows a 'barn' at the farm location.)

The Tithe Map of circa 1838 shows the owner of the lands around here as Lord Calthorpe, the Lord of the Manor of Acle. Area 675 is called Mill Marsh and area 668 is given as 'Barn and Yards', both occupied by Benjamin Heath Baker, while area 663 is given as 'Mill Hill & Mill' occupied by Robert England, and area 664 is occupied by Benjamin Rumbold.

The mills on the early 1797 and 1826 maps probably would have been quite primitive windmills of some sort. Of the two draining pumps shown on the 1880s and later maps the more eastern pump was a brick tower cloth-sailed windmill, and the west pump was a Steam Engine drainage pump.

A steam engine pump is said to have been built here by Holmes & Sons of Norwich in about 1878 and was a double-crank compound engine. An earlier steam engine was probably sited here since the 1861 census list 'Steam Mill' as the residence of Mr Rumbold.

(A.C. Smith says there is an old mill site about here with 'no remains visible', and suggests there may have been a trestle mill in the early days.)

From the Acle census returns we find the following are probably living at 'Marsh Farm', and the marshmen listed below were probably responsible for tending the Calthorpe Level Acle Marsh Farm drainage pump:

1841: Benjamin Rumbold, 35, Ag Lab
1851: Entry 42, Marsh House: Benjamin Rumbold, 47 Farm Bailiff
1861: Entry 11 Steam Mill: Benjamin Rumbold, 57, marshman,
And Entry 12 Steam Mill: James Allen. Ag Lab.
1871: Entry 14 Near Stokesby Wall: Benjamin Rumbold, 67, Marshman,
And Benjamin Rumbold, 44, marshman.
1881: Entry : Benjamin Rumbold, 77, Farm Bailiff.
1891: Entry 199: Marsh Wall: William Halesworth, marshman
1901: Entry 197: Near Steam Mill: William Halesworth, 69, marsh labourer, born Reedham, and then a dwelling empty.

MUCKFLEET TG421105

This marks the boundary between the old East and West Flegg Hundreds, and between Stokesby and Burgh St Margaret parishes. It runs for about 2.5 miles to Filby Broad. It was once navigatable by small craft and it is believed to get its name from craft carrying muck from Yarmouth to fertilize the agricultural lands in the neighbouring areas.

On the east side of the Muckfleet there was at TG434124 on Bryant's map of 1826 a mill marked as '**Stokesby Mill**'. It was not marked on Faden's map and is not shown on the 1996 map. Several other drainage pumps were once located along the length of the Muckfleet and the New Muckfleet Drain.

MUCKFLEET ELECTRIC PUMP TG421105

This is shown at the junction of the Muckfleet with the River Bure on the 1996 OS map. Nothing was shown on the 1951 OS map at this location and a sluice only was shown here on the 1880s OS map.

The pump here was constructed in the late 1970s and was commissioned in 1980. It consists of two Archimedes Screw type pumps pumping upto a total of 80 tones a minute. It cost £287,000 with the new drains. The pump drains about 773 hectares of the former Stokesby, Clippesby, Great Winkle and Muckfleet levels.

ACLE BOAT DYKE TG413406

This runs in a westerly direction for about ¼ mile towards the Hermitage public house. The Benns family lived near the dyke during the nineteenth century and were coal merchants who had wherries.

Before the building of the roads and railways, transport was mainly by river and wherries were the main craft during the nineteenth century. At the end of the Acle dyke is a staithe where wherry cargos were loaded and unloaded. Some wherry owners at Acle include: Robert Newby was listed in 1836 as a wherry owner at Acle and Joshua Mallett, at the Angel was listed as a wherry owner in 1864.

Today Russell Marine has the Acle Marina on the Acle Boat Dyke. Established in 1984 this is for private boats and can accommodate up to 150 boats.

Bryan Banham today runs a Plant and Machinery Leasing business at Broad Farm on Boat Dyke Lane.

BOAT DYKE PUMP

An electric pump which could lift 40 tons of water per minute was built at TG409107 next to the Acle Dyke in 1949.

More WHERRIES & Wherrymen from elsewhere:
The Acle census returns list several wherries moored at Acle Boat Dyke, many of them containing whole families. Some of the wherries and wherrymen listed were:
1901 census:
Entry 208: Wherry '**Louisa**' at Boat Dyke; William Harding, 40, Wherryman
Entry 209: Wherry '**Zeph**' at Boat Dyke; Benjamin Bessey, 67, Wherryman
1881 census:
Vessel "**Matilda**"
Samuel Cornham , 53, wherryman bn Neatishead
Robert Page, 28, wherryman mate bn Gt. Yarmouth
Vessel "**Zulu**"

John H. Money, 37, wherryman Bn Coltishall
John M. Money, 10, wherryman
Vessel "**Arthur**"
William Clarke, 59, wherryman bn Upton
Vessel "**Henry**"
George Roper, 36, wherryman bn Worstead
Vessel "**Woodman**"
Robert Bates, 26, wherryman bn Stalam
Dennis Bates, 21, wherryman mate
Vessel "**Bure**"
Robert Bircham, 40, wherryman bn Norfolk
1871 census:
'**GEORGE**' of Norwich, a 23 ton wherry of corn, William Parker, 62, master born Plumstead
'**VIOLET**' of Oxnead, a 16 ton wherry of coal & corn, Isaac Bussey?, 26, bn Plumstead
'**ONWARD**' of Somerton, a 15 ton wherry of corn, Robert Powley, 26, master, bn Tunstall
'**WIDGEON**' of Wroxham, a 22 ton wherry of coal & brick, William Southgate, 71?, master bn Horning

HERMITAGE PUBLIC HOUSE TG408106

This is located near the end of Acle Dyke at TG 408106 close to Old Road, the A1064 road.
It was shown at area 328 on the Acle Tithe Map of 1838 as '**HERMITAGE INN**', owned by Edmund Lacon and occupied by Joseph Bane or Hunn.

Hermitage Public House near Acle Dyke.

Faden's 1797 map shows the '**SHIP**' near the roadway and 'Hermitage' near the Dyke, possibly suggesting that the pub was at one time called the Ship and the Hermitage was another building at that time. Bryant's map of 1826 does not mark the Hermitage but has the '**PRINCE OF WALES INN**' marked near where the pub now stands. So it is possible that the Hermitage Inn had both of these names before becoming the Hermitage and that the Hermitage of 1797 was not a public house but perhaps another building.

BLOFIELD & WALSHAM LICENCE REGISTERS list some owners of the Hermitage as LACONS, and WHITBREAD to closure 1978. When it reopened in 1985 it was called **REBA'S RIVERSIDE INN**. It is marked on the 1996 OS map as **Riverside Inn.**

It was renamed the **Hermitage** by September 2003

It was an Alehouse originally and later had a full licence.

Occupant	Comments / Notes	Date
THOMAS KENDALL		1836
JOSEPH BANE or HUNN!	Surname not clear!	1838
JOSEPH HUNN	1841 listed as Innkeeper **P. of Wales**. 1845 listed as Victualler & thatcher.	1841
WILLIAM BENNS	Listed at 'Hermitage' but as a waterman and not as licensee!	1851
JAMES HUNN	Listed in 1851, age 37, as Innkeeper on Old Road (entry 89) but place not named! Listed here 1854 directory.	1851 - 1896
JAMES BARBER	Fine £1 plus 9/6d costs or 28 days detention for keeping open during prohibited hours - 02.11.1896	09.02.1896
EDWARD READ		12.07.1897
HARRY RICHARD SHALDERS		16.03.1903
SAMUEL CHARLES THAXTER	Listed in 1908	02.01.1905
GEORGE CHRISTMAS SMITH	Listed in 1916&1922	15.01.1912
RALPH RANOLD PEARMAN		01.10.1931
REGINALD CHARLES SMITH		27.11.1933
PERCY HENRY NICHOLS		09.08.1943 to 1974+

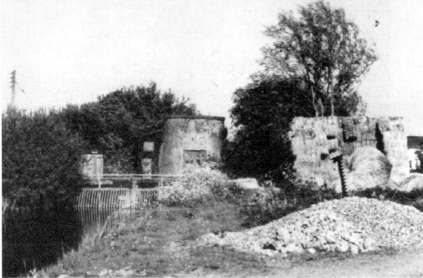

Charlie Water's Mill. Top in 1938. Bottom in 1989 AC Smith.

111

CHARLIE WATER'S MILL. TG413110

This is on the west side of the river, located on the Hermitage Marshes near to Mill House Farm in the Acle parish.

A mill was shown here on Faden's Map of 1797, on the 1799 Acle Enclosure map on 'Bridge Marshes' owned by T.B. Burroughs, and on Bryant's 1826 Map. It was not shown on the 1st Edition OS map but was marked on the Acle Tithe Map. Henry Negus Burroughes was shown as the 'owner and occupier' of area 312 called 'Mill Hill & Yards' on the 1838 Tithe Map.

It was marked as a 'Draining Pump' on the 1884 and 1950s OS maps.

A. C. Smith described it, in 1989, as a derelict redbrick tower stump of 2 storeys high with a flat roof, double doors and windows, and used at that time as a store. It had once driven a scoopwheel. Rex Wailes called this Thrigby Charlie Water's Mill and believes the millwright was Smithdale

Some probable marshman who operated the mill and pump include:

1861 census entry 18 Marsh House: Edward Jackson, marshman
1871 census entry 21, Old Yarmouth Rd Marsh House: Edward Jackson, 50, marshman.
1881 census: Edward Jackson, 66, marshman
1891 census entry 204, Yarmouth Old Road: John Wisken, 40 marshman.
1901 census entry 74, Bridge Road: George Green, 32, marshman.

GREAT WINKLE LEVEL PUMP TG416114

On the 1880s OS map a 'draining pump' was marked at this location on the east side of the river in the Burgh St Margaret's parish. This was also shown on the 1950s OS map, and the 1996 OS map also shows a drainage pump here. The marshes here were called the Great Winkle Level. Rex Wailes says a tower mill was located at TG416114 and named it as **FLEGGBURGH MILL** or **BILLOCKBY MILL**. He gives the millwright as WT England and says the mill had patent sails and drove a 17ft 6in diameter scoopwheel and drained 394 acres.

There was no pump shown at this location on the 1797, 1826 or 1st edition OS map of the 1830s.

On the Tithe map of 1838 no pump is marked here, but nearby, at TG416115, on the area listed as 424 a house, barn and stable are marked owned by James Conway Travers and occupied by William Porter. This house was shown on Faden's1797 map as 'Marsh House' and on the 1826 Bryant's map as '**Acle Bridge Farm**'. The house was marked on the 1996 OS map as '**Bridge Farm**'.

The 1902 Altered Tithe Map shows this house and premises are now occupied and owned by Charles Belgrave Lucas and a drainage pump is located at the junction of areas numbered 91 and 96 and is also owned by Lucas.

In July 1919 when the Filby Estate went up for sale at auction by direction of C. B. Lucas the drainage pump was part of lot 38 described as:

Valuable Marsh Farm and Mill conveniently situate abutting the river, close to Acle Bridge where during the summer months a considerable trade can be done in poultry and dairy produce; in all containing by the OS 13a 0r 33p or thereabouts, now in the occupation of Mr W. C. Saunders, a yearly tenant, at the apportioned rent of £27 10s 0d. There is a brick and tiled house containing Entrance lobby, Sitting Room, Kitchen, Dairy, Pantry, and 3 Bedrooms; adjoining being a Wash-house and other offices. Cow-house for 4 beasts with loose box, Calves Crib and a Hay-house adjoining; Yard with Lodge Piggeries, Garden, Orchard and 2 Marshes adjoining. A Corrugated Iron DRAINAGE MILL containing a 6 h.p. Horizontal Boiler by Robey & Co., and Engine and Turbine by Smithdale & Sons, with Coal House adjoining.
The drainage rates receivable in respect of the mill will be £66 10s 6d.

The Tubby family were at Bridge farm in the 1940s and Sidney Hewitt was the marshman here later. Mr Alan Hobbs became the owner of Bridge Farm and the premises are now occupied by Acle Electrical Testing.

ACLE PRIORY TG413115

An Augustinian Priory was founded by Roger Bigod near the Bridge Inn in the late 13th century and was known as Weybridge Priory. It was dedicated to Saint Mary. The Priory closed in 1536 and there are now little visible remains of the Priory but the area is now considered as an ancient monument.
(The 1845 directory incorrectly placed the Priory 'a short distant east of the Church', and the 1880s OS map also placed the Priory close to the Acle Church.)

BRIDGE INN TG414116

This is located close to Acle Bridge, and dates from about 1460 – 1480. It has been known by several names including: **ANGEL, ANGEL INN**, **ANGEL & BRIDGE HOUSE**, **BRIDGE** or **BRIDGE HOUSE**, and **BRIDGE HOTEL**.
It was an Alehouse.
Some Owners include: Henry Negus Burroughs, and later his trustees. MORGANS took over from 21.11.1921. STEWARD & PATTESON on 1 October 1961, and WATNEY MANN from 21 February 1967. In the 1990s the owners were Grand Metropolitan Estates Ltd.
It is currently owned by the Maypole Group and the general managers are Phil & Vanessa Hannon.

Occupant / licensee	Comments	Date
BENJAMIN PORTER	Age 75 in 1841 Victualler and lime burner in 1836	1836 - 1845
GEORGE BOND	age 30 in 1851	1850 - 1851
JOSEPH MALLETT	Victualler	1854

GEORGE BOND		1856
JOSHUA MALLETT	Listed in 1864 as wherry owner, lime, tile, & brick merchant, victualler & coal merchant. Age 57 in 1871 census, born Gt. Yarmouth.	1858
EDWARD ROSE	1881 age 40 born Stumpshaw, innkeeper & coalmerchant. Age 60 in 1901. Listed as coal merchant & boat proprietor in 1896 & 1908	24.11.1879
THOMAS ALFRED SPURGEON GEORGE		06.11.1911
AGNES ANN GEORGE		11.01.1932
ALFRED PERRY		22.06.1936
WILLIAM FREDERICK HAYLES		07.01.1946
EDWARD MATTHEW NUGENT		25.05.1959
WILLIAM JOHN SPEED		06.05.1968 to 1974+

Bridge Inn, Acle in 2008.

ACLE BRIDGE TG414116

A bridge has existed here for about a thousand years.
The bridge was marked on the 1797 map as '**Wey Bridge**'.
The old Yarmouth road, now the A1064, crosses the river here.

Top: Acle Bridge from john Lubbock. Bottom: Pan-Aero aerial postcard view of Acle Bridge in the 1930s showing the Bridge Inn and Eastwick's boatyard.

A 3 arch stone bridge was built here around 1830. The maximum clearance under the central arch was 9 ft. at the centre at high water. The two piers of the bridge were supported on oak wood piles.

A single arch bridge was built in the early 1930s. The Norfolk County Council in 1928 proposed that the 3 arch bridge should be replaced with a single arch bridge which was to provide a high water clearance at the centre of 12 ft. The roadway was to be 30 ft wide and a 5 ft wide path was provided at either side. To accommodate the road traffic during the bridge demolition and rebuilding a temporary bridge was constructed on the Yarmouth side of the bridge. The temporary bridge, designed by Christiani Nielsen of London, provided a 10 foot wide roadway with a 4 foot wide walkway. It was constructed on waling and piles with RSJs supporting 8" x 4" timber decking, which was topped with 9" x 3" deals.

The present bridge was built 1997 at a cost of £1,600,000. Clearance under the present bridge is 3.66m (12 ft.) at high water.

ACLE BRIDGE STORES

This was started by Mr Ernest Noah Curtis in the 1920s. It was taken over by Gordon Curtis and later by Mr & Mrs Frank Howard and Janet Howard nee Curtis. The Howard family still owned the land here when the new Acle Bridge was built.

ACLE REGATTA

The first Acle Regatta was in 1890 with a reported 150 yachts taking part.
This takes place on the stretch of river upstream of Acle Bridge.
After many years absence the regatta was restarted in 1978.

ACLE BOATYARDS

A staithe was marked on the1880s OS map on the south side of the river immediately upstream of the Acle Bridge. In the 1904 directory an Edward Howes of the Prospect Brick Works of Sprowston was listed as a brick maker with a place at Acle Bridge. It is probable that the company used the staithe here.

John Walter Eastwick started a boatbuilding business here in the early twentieth century. He was listed in 1916 and 1922 as a boat-builder and in 1933 as a yacht agent.

Mr Grottick ran the boatyard and the yard became Sunboats. Grottick still owned land here when the new Acle Bridge was built.

Another boatyard appeared later and was usually referred to as Alan Johnsons Boatyard, also known as Faircraft. In the 1990s it was owned by Broads Tours Ltd of Wroxham and leased to Mr and Mrs Foley.
Horizon Craft, part of Horning Pleasurecraft Ltd, now operate from Acle Bridge.

116

MAURICE WINTER REMEMBERS

The furthest back that I can remember is 1930. There is a place on the right bank of the River Bure, about half way between Acle Bridge and Upton Dyke, where the rond loops a short distance away from the river to leave a strip of land between the rond and the river. This strip is a foot or so below the level of the top of the rond. My father leased a plot on this strip of land from Mr. Key, the farmer who owned the adjacent marshes.

Dad, and a colleague of his at the office where they worked, called Harry, collaborated to build some little huts on the plot, so that it could be used as a weekend retreat, and for short holidays. All constructions were in wood. They fenced off the plot first. Then they built a small hut and put a paraffin stove in it, to use as a kitchen. They cut two small dykes, one at the downstream end, and the other at the upstream end of the plot. There then followed the main hut, for use as a living room, dining room and bedroom, a wet boat house over the upstream dyke, and a long narrow hut at the back of the plot, with a workshop in one end and a small bedroom in the other end. At the head of the upstream dyke they excavated a basin, and made a slipway of wood. The rond was outside the plot, and was, of course, left intact, as any breach of it would have resulted in the marshes being flooded, as most of the time they were below river level.

As the work progressed Mum and Dad and myself (I was an only child), went to stay at our place by the river at weekends. I helped with the creosoting of the timber. I got covered in creosote, which Dad cleaned off me when we got home. If today's Health and Safety people could have seen what we got up to, they would have had forty fits!! It was tremendous fun and we all enjoyed it immensely.

Dad and Harry bought several small boats which they kept in the dykes or the boat house. There was one little boat that I loved particularly, a river skiff. It had one rowing seat, and a seat in the stern from where the boat could be steered with rudder strings. She was not typical of the Bure, most people had tubby little dinghies for pottering about, the skiff was narrower in the beam, and beautifully streamlined in her underwater shape, thereby being much easier and faster to row. My father must have bought her second hand, she was definitely not new. Of course we had to be careful with her, or you could turn her over. Our first outings in the skiff were with Dad rowing, Mum in the stern, steering, and me crouching on the floor board in the bows (I was still quite a small child at that time). This arrangement balanced the boat nicely. We would often go down river as far as Acle Bridge to buy provisions. On the left side of the river (as viewed looking downstream), just on the upstream side of the Bridge, were two provision shops. The one nearer the Bridge was run by a Mrs. Gray, the other, next door, was rather larger, run by a family by the name of Curtis. My parents would favour Mrs. Gray's, and we would stock up with all sorts of goodies. The Curtis family ran two motor boats that were loaded with supplies, these would ply up and down the river selling to people on moored boats. They sent one boat early in the mornings up to Potter Heigham, and they would sell their goods to boat people there. One of the boats was called "Our Boys", and I saw that craft many many years later preserved in the Museum of the Broads.

Riverside Chalet in the 1930s built by the Winter family, supplied by Maurice J. Winter.

On the right bank of the river, opposite the provision shops, was Mr. Grottick's boatyard. Dad used to go there for supplies of paint, paraffin and suchlike. Quite often Dad and I would go to the Yard in the boat – much easier and quicker than walking – to pick up various items. I would steer, and out of devilment I would zigzag all over the river. Dad said I was leading him a dance. He got fed up with that, and overcame my steering with extra pressure on the oars to keep the boat straight. He drummed it into me that I must keep to the right – that was when I learnt that when afloat, you pass on the opposite side to what you do on the road.

One day, Dad needed to go to Grottick's for something, and I went with him, steering. It was a nasty day, it had been raining, was dull overcast, and blowing a gale from the north east. Dad instructed me to head into Grottick's dyke, which was at right angles to the river. The dyke had Grottick's boats moored either side, which left very little room for the boat, with the oars sticking out either side. Dad had to withdraw the oars inboard somewhat, leaving less length outboard. This made the boat very difficult to control, with the gale directly behind it pushing it forward fast.

Mr. Grottick appeared on the scene, apparently in a state of great agitation. He was afraid that we were going to collide with and scratch his beautiful boats. He ran round the head of the dyke, to get to the other side, but slipped on the wet duckboards, and fell into the dyke. He disappeared from my view behind a moored speedboat; I said to Dad "Mr. Grottick's fallen in", but Dad was too busy struggling with boat to pay much heed to what I said. A moment later, Mr. Grottick reappeared, and climbed onto the bank. He was not at all pleased. It was very lucky that he did not hit his head on the speedboat; if he had, he would have been a hospital case. Dad and I got ashore, and found Mr. Grottick in a foul temper, he roundly berated my father, saying "A man of your experience should know better than to attempt to enter the dyke in these conditions". Mr. Grottick was right, of course, Dad should have known better. Dad went to see Bill Suffling, Mr. Grottick's assistant, about whatever business had brought us there. Bill Suffling thought that it was a huge joke that his employer had fallen into the water, and could not stop laughing!

We continued to visit our place by the river during my childhood in the thirties. We were always glad to get there, we had big appetites, which we put down to the invigorating effect of the clean country air. Of course, it may have been because we were very active and so happy. We made a lawn in front of the main hut, and flower beds around the borders – the flowers grew with great vigour and brilliant colours.

Maurice Winter in the river skiff in 1936, supplied by Maurice J. Winter.

My bedroom was in the long hut at the back of the plot, accessed via the workshop. On quiet nights I would sometimes hear a rhythmic deep booming noise, just at the limit of audibility. I was to learn later that it was the Cross Sand Light Vessel sounding her fog horn, and that the sound travelled a long distance when there was calm still warm air overlying a cooler surface. I could also hear birds chattering in the reeds, I think they must have been reed warblers, sounding "churr churr churr, sss churr" and so on. I used to imagine that they were arguing incessantly with their wives. One morning in high summer, when I had woken very early, it was very warm, sun shining strongly, and I got up, removed my pyjamas, and stepped outside, stark naked in the sunshine. Nobody else was about, then I heard "clink clink clink clink". It was a wherry coming very slowly in the light breeze upstream from Acle Bridge, she was hoisting her sail after having shot the bridge. She continued on her way upstream.

On one occasion Dad took me into a little brick built pump house, with a tall chimney, near the bank just under a quarter of a mile downstream from our place. He said the pump was used to drain the marshes. It was driven by an internal combustion engine, I suppose its fuel must have been diesel, or possibly TVO (tractor vaporising oil). There was also an old redundant steam engine that used to drive the pump before the oil engine was installed.

Mr. Key, the farmer who owned the marshes behind us, employed a marshman by the name of Mr. Green. When he was on his rounds looking after the marshes, he would occasionally pay us a visit to see how we were getting on. He and my father would have a mardle.

My especial interest was the little river skiff, and before long Dad thought it was time that I learnt to row. I was sat in the rowing seat, the oars were put into my little hands, and I was made to row. I took to it at once, and absolutely loved it. After a while, I was allowed to go solo in the boat, subject to very strict instructions as to where and how far I could go. Some great crested grebes lived in the river nearby, and I used to watch them fishing when I rowed near to them. I used to note the direction in which the bird was pointing when it dived, and row to where I thought it would surface, but I was always wrong – the grebe must have turned this way and that under water in pursuit of its prey. From time to time the steam ship "Queen of the Broads" would pass by, her deck would be crowded with passengers. She was a lovely old vessel, now, sadly, broken up. I kept well out of her way, but I loved to feel the motion of the boat bouncing up and down in her wash. I would turn her bows into the wash, as I had been taught, then "sploosh, sploosh, sploosh". Games like these taught me how to manoeuvre the boat quickly and easily, a skill which was to stand me in good stead in later years. That skiff also imbued me with a love of boats and the water, which lasted to this day, and led on to other things, but that is another story. I became like Ratty in the "Wind in the Willows", always happy when I "was messing about in boats".

My earliest recollection of the Wey Bridge is that it was a three span structure, with two piers standing in the river to support it. This bridge was removed, and replaced by the current single span structure. Exactly which year that occurred I do not know, but I should think it must have been around 1930. After the new bridge was built, my parents observed that the tidal flows past our riverside plot were stronger than before, presumably the supporting piers had acted like a brake on the flow of water.

One hot sunny day when we were tending the riverside garden, we saw that the reeds on the opposite bank were being blown flat. Dad said that a "Roger Blast" was coming, and in a moment, the wind blew at gale force for about 15 seconds, it then moved away over the marshes. I have since learnt that these blasts tend to occur over the marshes in hot still weather.

I used to row the little skiff up as far as a mill about a quarter of a mile downstream from the mouth of Upton Dyke, and on the opposite bank. If I had more time and Dad allowed it, I would row up to the head of Upton Dyke; I would be solo in the boat for these trips. The Dyke was reed fringed on both sides. The head of the Dyke opened out, as it does now, to give room for turning. There was an earth slipway at the very end of the dyke, but I never attempted to land. From where I sat in the boat, I could see no habitation, nor any sign of life. As time went on, and I became stronger and more competent, I used to row further up the river from time to time.

After a few years, Grottick's Yard reinvented itself as "Sunboats". They had a fleet of motor cruisers, all with "Sun" in their name, like Desert Sun, Morning Sun, etc. Bill Suffling had taken over from Mr. Grottick. They had excavated a basin, between the river bank and the boatshed, in which the cruisers were kept, the basin connected with the river by a short dyke.

The years of the thirties went by; then the War came. Dad sub-let the plot to a couple who were going to live there, and we never visited the place again.

Many years rolled by when I had little or no contact with the River Bure. In 1982 or 1983, I went to Upton Dyke in order to help a friend of mine to refit a second hand sailing cruiser that he had bought. The place had changed totally. Eastwood Whelpton Boatyard had been established, and my friend had put his boat there. This yard was one of the few on the Broads where they would allow you to work on your boat while it was stored there. The Yard is run by Tim and Anne Whelpton. They have a team of boat builders who have created a fleet of beautiful sailing cruisers for hire. A boatwright by the name of Peter Simpson runs a one man business from a workshop situated in the Yard. The Dyke has lost its reed fringes, and has been piled; there is a wooden slipway where it had been bare earth. Boats are moored all along one side of the Dyke. The Yard also built a craft for the purpose of securing the sailing speed record. I went down the towpath as far as the main river, from where I could see the mill on the opposite bank; it had fallen into a state of decrepitude. A year or two later when the refit of my friend's boat was complete, we cruised down the Bure past what had been our riverside plot. All the constructions that Harry and my father had built had disappeared, the dykes had been filled in; there were no boats, just a small hut had been built at the back of the plot. There was no sign of life. Rather sad, after the happy times we had had there.

On my bookshelf I have a Hamilton's "Broads Navigation" that I had forgotten I had. It is dated 1953. The pump house that my father took me into is clearly marked; access to it appears to be via the tow path. No other pump or mill is shown in the vicinity. On the other side of the river, it shows the mill that I mentioned earlier, a little way downstream from Upton Dyke; it also shows a steam or motor driven pump close on the downstream side of the mill. Access to both of those structures is shown as by the tow path. Hamilton names the reaches upstream and downstream of the mill, as Upper Davey's Mill Reach, and Lower Davey's Mill Reach.

Hamilton mentions two Boatyards at Acle Bridge, Sunboats, and Eastick's Ltd. He also mentions "Curtis Bridge Stores", but not Gray's provision shop.

Hamilton mentions two bungalows with private moorings; one of these was ours, and the other, I remember Dad said, belonged to a Mr. Bonner. I do not remember if Bonner's bungalow was still there when we cruised down river. Hamilton mentions good moorings at Upton Dyke, with access to Upton Village, but says nothing about Eastwood Whelpton Boatyard, so I suppose that had not been built at that time.

121

ST MARGARET'S MILL TG418119

This was in the parish of Burgh St Margaret, also known as Fleggburgh or Burgh. It is located on the east side of the A1064.

The mill was not marked on Faden's map but was marked as **'Burgh Mill'** on Bryant's map. The OS map of circa 1884 marks it simply as a 'draining pump'. It is marked on the 1996 OS map as **'Fleggburgh Drainage mill'**

Rex Wailes called it **'Acle WeyBridge mill'**, and AC Smith called it **'Fleggburgh Mill'**.

AC Smith writing in 1989 described the mill as 'a white painted tower of 4 storeys high with a glazed top and black timber roof with a large building attached and converted into a restaurant'. Earlier he had described the mill as a converted tarred red brick tower.

The mill became a private residence in the 1960s and a restaurant in the 1970s. In September 2002 the converted mill and attached buildings with 4.5 acres of ground was advertised for sale at offers in the region of £395,000. In June 2004 it was again advertised for sale with a price of £425,000. It is now know as St Margarets Mill Retreat and is occupied by Kevin Daniels who runs an Holistic Centre here and provides bed and breakfast accommodation. Mr Daniels also runs Ha-Ra Daniels UK Ltd, providing biodegradable cleaning products, and Aglaia Body Care Products from the premises.

A mill was located here from at least 1801 since the 'Inclosure State of The Claims' of 21st July 1801 list 'Marsh House Mill & 40 acres in Burgh' in the occupation of John Hollis and owned by James Symonds

The Burgh & Billockby Drainage Commission met for the first time on 7th May 1804 and the meeting notes refer to the 'new mill' suggesting it had only recently been built. John Hollis was the millman at that time. The mill then was a small cloth-sailed mill as the meeting notes of 13th May 1814 says 'the mill needs 2 new cloth sails'. In 1821 the millwright Mr Henry Lock of Norwich was asked to make a new scoopwheel, and in 1837 Stolworthy was asked to do some repairs to the mill.

On the Tithe Map circa 1838 the mill is marked on area 396. The owner is put as the Commissioners of Drainage and the occupier as Carmi Hollis. The nearby house & garden on area 394 was owned by Thomas Daniels and occupied by Mr Golder.

In 1839 William Porter became the millman, taking over from John Hollis. William Porter was shown on the Tithe map as the occupant area 424 'House, Barn & Stable' next to the river. This is the property now known as **'Bridge Farm'** located at about TG416115.

In 1840 the mill was damaged during a storm.

In 1841 a new tower was to be 'erected on the foundations of the old mill at the top of the door'. Edward Smith, a bricklayer of Stokesby was asked to do the brickwork for £50, and Robert and James Stolworthy were asked to convert the mill to 'self-acting winding tackle with patent sails' for a fee of £219.

In the 1870s a portable steam engine was employed to drive the scoopwheel and in 1874 a small building was erected to facilitate a portable steam engine. The contract to drain the marshes with a portable steam engine was awarded annually and in 1877 Mr George Bond had the contract and was paid £40 for the year.
Daniel Rust did some repairs to the mill in 1876.

In 1879 the Drainage Commission decided to purchase their own steam engine for a sum of £93-5s-3d. John Debbage became the millman and worked the steam engine during the 1880s. His son Walter Debbage also worked the steam engine. (The mill was probably used till the 1930s)

Some marshmen listed in the censuses and directories for Burgh St Margaret / Fleggburgh who may have worked this drainage pump, and perhaps the Great Winkle Level pump, include:

1891 census: Entry 68 Common: George Green, 48, marshman and his son, George Green, 20 marshman.
1901 census: Entry 130 Causeway: John Debbage, 76.
                 Entry 131 Causeway: Walter Debbage, 44
                 Entry 132 George Green, 58 and Walter Bland, 17
1896 directory John Debbage, marshfarmer
1908, 1916 & 1925 directories: Walter Debbage, marshfarmer.

**St Margaret's Mill in working order from a Valentines Post Card.
Peter Allard Collection.**

St Margaret's or Fleggburgh Mill:
Top left circa 1960 from Mike Pickard, Top right 1973 from AC Smith and Bottom in 2002.

FISHLEY MILL TG410117

'FISHLEY MILL', lying to the south of the river, on Fishley Marshes, was shown with this name on Bryant's 1826 map.

A mill was shown at about this location on the earlier 1797 Faden's map marked as 'Drain W Mill'. The 1st edition OS map of 1830's also shows a mill at this approximate location.

A mill was also shown on the 1838 Tithe map at area 19, listed as 'Garden with site of Mill'. The owner was Rev Edward Marsham and the occupier was given as Elizabeth Taylor.

The circa 1880s OS map shows a 'draining pump' much further to the west at about TG407117, suggesting the earlier mill had been demolished and a new pump built. This pump was a steam engine pump which was later replaced with a diesel pump. The pump was also shown here on the circa 1950 OS map.

A.C. Smith indicates 'an old site with no remains' at this approximate location.

The 1996 OS map shows nothing at either of these locations.

Fishley Mill, Acle

Postcard showing the Fishley Steam Drainage Pump. Peter Allard Collection

CLIPPESBY MILL TG409128

A mill was marked here on the east side of the river on the 1797 map as a 'Drain Mill' along with a nearby marsh house. It was shown on the 1826 map as **'Clippesby Mill'**, although it is located in the parish of Ashby with Oby.

It was shown on the Ashby & Oby Tithe Map at area 233 labelled as 'Mill & Yard', owned by Henry Muskett, the Lord of the Manor of Clippesby, hence the name of the mill. It was occupied by William Davey according to the Tithe Apportionment of that time. The adjacent area 235 was labelled as 'Cottage and Yard' and was also occupied by William Davey.

The marshmen who tended this mill were listed in the Ashby with Oby censuses. The above mentioned William Davey was listed in the 1851 Ashby with Oby census returns as age 37, carpenter.

This is a red brick tower mill, 4 storeys high, 41 feet to the top of the cap. It drove a scoopwheel. It has probably been hained at some point in time. A date of 1814 is marked inside, so the mill of 1797 may have been a different earlier construction. The earlier mills would have had cloth sails but in the later years it had patent sails.

The cap was boatshaped and it had a gallery and petticoat. The tower diameter at the base was 21 feet and 13 feet at the top. The walls at the base are 3 foot thick. It had 2 doors on the ground floor and one window on each of the first and second floors.

There was a fireplace on the ground floor. Rex Wailes believes it was lived in and the ceilings were rushed and plastered.

There is a brick pumphouse nearby.

William Hewitt was the marshman here for a time in the mid twentieth century.

The mill became a holiday home in about 1958.

It was struck by lightening in 1978 and the stocks were then removed.

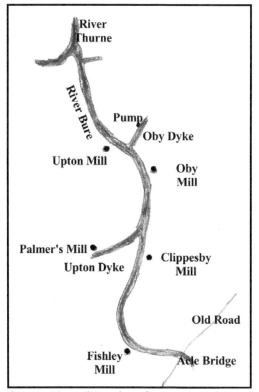

Sketch Map of the river from Acle Bridge to the River Thurne.

Clippesby Mill. Top: 1930, bottom April 1982. Peter Allard Collection.

Clippesby Mill in 1973 from AC Smith

UPTON DYKE TG408131

This dyke runs for about 0.4 mile from the west side of the river Bure in a WSW direction. The Eastwood Whelpton boatyard is on the dyke at Upton Yacht Station. This was established by Tim and Anne Whelpton in the 1950s. They are boatbuilders and boat hirers and provide sailing yachts for charter hire and rowing boats. The Norfolk Broads School of Sailing run RYA sailing courses from the Upton Yacht Station.

Clippesby Mill in 1987 AC Smith

PALMER'S MILL TG403129

This is located on Upton Dyke and was rebuilt here by Sego between 1977 and 1980.
It was originally located at TG405102 in Acle till 1976.
At Acle it was originally a hollow post mill with a plunger pump and the original millwrights are believed to have been Whitmore and Binyon but it was later rebuilt by Smithdale. It had spring sails and twin winding tails.

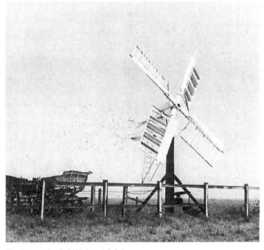

Palmer's Mill in 1981

OBY MILL TG409138

This was a 4 storey red brick tower mill on the east side of the river in the parish of Ashby with Oby. It was marked as a 'drain mill' in 1797, as OBY MILL on Bryant's map of 1826 and is marked on all subsequent maps. The 1884 and 1892 OS maps indicate a **ferry** crossing here next to the mill. It is probable that this was nothing more than a rowing boat.

On the Ashby & Oby Tithe Map, circa 1840, area 224 is labelled as 'Mill & Yard' owned by Ann Cremer and occupied by John Wiseman. The adjacent area 225 is 'Cottage & Garden owned by Ann Cremer an occupied by Daniel Broom.
Daniel Broom was listed in the 1841 census, and then again in the 1851 census at entry 4 'Oby On The Marshes' as a 56 year old marshman, and he was probably responsible for tending to this mill.

Oby Mill in working order Peter Allard Collection

The mill is often called **WISEMAN'S MILL**. The Wiseman family were farmers in the parish, and in the 1891 census returns Alfred B. Wiseman, age 33, was the tenant farmer at Oby Hall. The Oby Manor estate was the property of the Wyndham Cremer family. In the Norfolk Chronicle of 10th June 1905 the estate was put up for sale: *'Sewell & Brereton have received instructions from Mrs T. Wyndham*

Cremer to sell by auction at the Royal Hotel, Norwich on Saturday July 8, 1905 at 3.30 in the afternoon precisely all that very desirable FREEHOLD PROPERTY situate 3 miles from Acle and Marham Stations and known as MANOR HOUSE ESTATE comprising a capital residence, commodious agricultural buildings, two brick and tile cottages, and 288a. 2r. 37p. of good deep soil Arable, Marsh and Pasture Land as now in the occupation of the executors of the late Mr A.B. Wiseman at a rental of £275 per annum. Marshman's Cottage and Outbuildings, Brick Tower Windmill, with a portable engine in shed used as an auxiliary, driving a powerful Turbine and draining in addition to the marshes of the farm about 300 acres, the dues from which will be included in the sales.'

Oby Mill. Left: circa 1960 Mike Pickard. Right: in June 1988 from AC Smith.

The mill is said to have been built originally in 1753 by millwright Robert Martin of Barsham Bridge or Beccles. At that time it must have been a primitive cloth sailed mill.

In later years it was converted to patent sails and drove a turbine pump.

The mill itself became derelict in the 1930s and the turbine pump was powered by a diesel engine, and A. C. Smith, writing in 1988, described the mill then as a derelict red brick tower of 4 storeys without a cap but with fan cradle, 2 sail stocks and spider, clasp-arm wooden brake-wheel, windshaft and all machinery inside including gears and shaft to the pump in the adjacent shed.

The fan cradle and stocks were removed in about 2000 and a tarpaulin cover was put on top of the tower. Millwright Richard Seago has done some work on the mill in recent years.

A recent photograph of Oby Mill

In 2008 the mill was put up for sale at auction with a guide price of £30,000 to £50,000 and was bought by Mr Adam Whiting for £41,500 in April 2008. It is currently a Grade II listed building.

The mill was also used for a time to drive a circular saw for cutting timber and the marshman here, William Davey, was listed as a carpenter in 1891.

Some of the marshmen listed in Oby with Ashby parish census returns that probably would have worked either this drainage pump or the Clippesby pump include the following:

1851 census: 'Oby on the marshes': Daniel Broom, 56, marshman, born Oby,
& William Davey, 37, carpenter.
1881 census: 'Marsh House': William Davey, 40, marshman,
& 'Marshfarm & Watermill': William Davey, 66, farmer 40 acres.
1891 census entry 61: William Davey, 50, carpenter.
1901 census: Entry 53, Marsh House: Frederick Debbage, 47, marshman, & Frederick Debbage, 25, marshman.
& Entry 54, Mill House: James Green, 39, farmer.
In the 1916, 1925 & 1937 Kelly's directories Harry Davey was listed as the marshman.
The Davey children went to the Upton School and had to be rowed across the river and then walk to the school every day.

SOUTH OBY DYKE TG407141

This runs in a roughly NNE direction from the east bank of the river Bure for about 1/5 mile. **OBY DYKE DRAINING PUMP** is marked on the 1996 OS map at about TG407143.

UPTON TALL MILL TG404141

This is shown on the 1996 OS map as Upton Tall Mill.
AC Smith called this **'Black Mill'** and Rex Wailes called it **'Tall Mill'**.

This is a converted black tarred red brick tower mill. It has 5 iron bands around the tower and once drove a turbine pump. The batter near the top changes and suggests it may have been hained or altered at sometime. Rex Wailes gives the millwright as Smithdale but a date of 1800 is marked by a window, suggesting it may have been much altered over the years. Richard Seago did some work on this mill in the more recent years.

An electric pump house now stands nearby and a steam pump house was also once located here.

A mill is shown here on the 1826 Bryant's map and on the Tithe map of circa 1839. The mill here at that time would have had a scoopwheel.

The Tithe Map shows area 258 as 'Mill & Yard, owned and occupied by the Commissioners of Drainage. The adjacent area 257 was listed as 'Mill House & Land' and was owned by the Commissioners of Drainage and occupied by George Willgrass.

George Willgrass was in the 1851 census listed as age 36, farm labourer, and in 1871 at entry 128 On the Marshes as 56, marshman, along with his son also George Willgrass 16, marshman. In 1891 William Willgrass is listed in Upton as a 37 year old marshman.

The marshman's dwelling near the mill was a bungalow and David Childs recalls that the Angel family was here in the 1930s and were followed by the Graves family. The property was later sold and it became a holiday home. When the electric pump nearby was built electric was laid on for the bungalow.

Upton Mill. Top left: in working order, top right: 5th September 2003, bottom 6th March 1983 with the old steam-pump building. Peter Allard Collection.

Upton Mill July 1987 from AC Smith

KEITH RACKHAM: SAILING ON THE BURE AND NORTH RIVERS IN THE 1950S.

Hellesdon Youth Club had a very active sailing group during the 1950s. At Easter we usually hired a couple of motor cruisers. We could then have a weekend on the Broads without having to go home at night. I think I may have had my first broads holiday at Easter 1949. I was an apprentice at Mann Egertons, Cromer Road, Norwich, and with two of the other lads there, Arthur and Terry, we would finish work on Good Friday at 5pm then get ourselves over to Wroxham as soon as possible to join up with others who had gone earlier to get the boats and were waiting, moored up near the bridge. This first trip was on boats from R. Moore & Sons; we had Rexmore, Seamore and Braemore with the lugsail dinghies that came them. We always had two or more boats, for sleeping arrangements, girls on one and boys on the other: mixed crews during the day. The youth club leader, Ralph Green, slept in the cockpit of the boys boat. Two of the girls were around 19 or 20 so they were in charge of the other boat.

I was 16 during 1949 so was not old enough to go to the pubs etc. not that I wanted to, after a day out on a boat in the chilly Easter breezes and all that fresh air we were all usually in bed before 10pm.

We cruised the Bure, Thurne and Ant at the Easter weekends and used dinghies to play in, when moored up for an hour or two for lunch and tea breaks.

Usually at bridge locations when we had to lower canopies, masts etc. to go underneath.

Easter 1950 at the Suspension Bridge Great Yarmouth. Keith Rackham.

As the summer went on we got into sailing in halfdeckers, which we hired from H.C. Banham, Percivals, and Chumley Hawkes yards at Horning. We had anything up to 5 or 6 boats out on a Sunday for our day out, sailing mainly on the Bure, down towards Acle, until it became turn back time. Sometimes we went up the Thurne. I recall that on one sunny morning we were making our way down river when somewhere near to St Bennets a motor cruiser and one of our halfdeckers misjudged things and an elderly lady got a bowsprit as an armrest as she took mid morning tea in her cabin. Names and boatyard details were exchanged and all was sorted out in a few minutes. Damage was well above the waterline so no one was sinking.

Sinking came along on another day. We had all of Banham's boats out, Clover I, Clover II and Thistle and maybe a lugsail or two. We had got as far as Acle Bridge and had moored moored up, bow on, to the soft area of bank away from the bridge. Topping lifts were deployed and the boats could stream off on just the bow rope. There were 4 or 5 boats in a row. In one next to mine they had got out the sandwiches and Corona and were happily enjoying lunch when we all saw that they were drifting away from the bank! The skipper for that day had tied down his mainsheet to stop the sail from flapping around too much. His crewman hadn't pushed in the rond anchor properly and before they could organise themselves to get under control a capricious gust of wind knocked the boat over so that it filled and sank within a few feet of the bank. We had to grab all the crew who were by now mostly in the water, two were hanging on to the mast and rigging and one had made it to the bank. We always had about 5 or 6 to a boat. So there we were, having to find up spare clothes to get the damp heroes dry and warm whilst somebody went to ring Banham's boatyard. They came along about an hour later in Bantab, Mr Banham's own big private boat. We had by then unshackled all we could reach at the top of the mast and collected all that had floated out of the boat. The halfdecker was over to one side with about four feet of the mast above water. The boatyard men used Bantab's boom as a crane to get things upright and then haul the stricken boat up to the surface where we could then bail it out. We had shared our food with the survivors whilst we had waited for the rescue. They then got taken back to Horning on Bantab with their halfdecker in tow.

Patricia Cousins and Patsy Howell by the Bridge Inn in 1952.
Keith Rackham.

I organised myself, when we had our two week summer holiday from Mann Egerton, with two of my mates from there and other youth club members, to hire a cabin cruiser from Banham's. During 1951 we had Harvest Moon a sailing only boat, in 1952 we had Silver Moon an auxiliary, at the insistence of my mate Colin Foster, who was engine mad. It didn't sail as well as Harvest Moon. However we had decent holidays on both and got to Oulton Broad, Hickling and Horsey during our weeks cruising and sailing. I also organised days out at weekends with other lads from work; we had lugsail halfdeckers out from Bob Applegates yard at Potter Heigham. I was hardly ever at home for a Sunday dinner for several years. Once we got the use of the Sea Cadets whaler and could keep it away from Foundry Bridge, I was sailing practically all year round. I've cleared snow out of the whaler to go for a sail on a broad somewhere.

Ken Baker ran a course at Stalham School where they built a boat from a kit, a 10 foot dinghy, which they named Adventure. From around 1952, spring, summer an autumn I was camping and sailing most weekends from Friday evening until Sunday.

Easter 1950 at Acle looking towards Upton. Keith Rackham.

By 1951 sailing courses were being run by the Central Council for Physical Recreation. At Easter and Whitsun we used Stalham School as a headquarters and hired halfdeckers from the yards at Horning and Potter Heigham. We even got to use Moores of Wroxham 'Rebel', a newly built halfdcker. We collected the boats on a Saturday and spent the day sailing them to Barton Broad, Cox Bros boatyard being our moorings for the duration of the course. During the week we made passage to Hickling where we left the boats at the Pleasure Boat Quay overnight and went back next day to make the trip back. We would also do a day trip to Ransworth and back. We never went much further than Thurne mouth as we did not want to leave our boats at Acle, nor Thurne Dyke overnight. At the end of the course we took the boats back to the various yards, with some of the students coming with us for an extra days sailing. When I arrived at Horning with mine it was discovered that we had left one boat behind at Barton. I volunteered to go and get it the next day, a Sunday. Next morning I set off early from Hellesdon on my Pedal cycle, with a days rations, and had another day of free sailing, with just me, my bike and a bag of sandwiches, arriving at Southgates yard late on Sunday afternoon.

Every year we had to bring the whaler back to Norwich for the Sea Cadets Annual inspection, by some Navel big wig, so that was a challenge when we kept it at Barton. Ken Baker and I were the only ones available for the whole weekend during 1951, therefore on the Friday evening we went to Barton Staithe in the County Council three tonner, which Ken had the use of. We slept in the back of this and were up early next morning to get under ay for a long two day trip to Norwich. We made it across Breydon and up to Reedham before nightfall, camping on the marsh near the upper end of the New Cut, below the Swing Bridge, overnight. Next day, Norwich, two long days in a sail only boat. From then on we kept the whaler on the Yare, first at Reedham and then Berney Arms. From 1952 the CCPR ran the summer courses at Berney Arms. The halfdeckers were delivered there by the boatyards. It would have taken too long for us to have collected them from Horning and Potter Heigham ourselves, negotiating the lower reaches of the Bure, Yarmouth Harbour and Breydon with the strong tides would have called for early accurate timing, which is not something you can rely on in a sail only boat.

July 1951 at Acle. Keith Rackham.

I recall our youth club Easter trip when we had the halfdeckers with us. We had moored overnight at the Yacht Station in Great Yarmouth, this would have been 1950, I think. We were scuttling about around midnight having to slacken off our moorings to keep our boats in the river. The tide and wind was such that the ebb had been held back and the quay was underwater by over a foot. The mooring bollards were under water, we used the dinghies to row around on the quay to get at them. The recent North Sea surges are nothing new!

By 1953, at the age of 20, I had interests in other things and had met the young lady who was to become my wife. On the Easter or Whitsun course that year she came with me on the collection day when we sailed from Horning to Barton. We always stopped above Ludham Bridge where we all met up after negotiating the bridge. We then went along to the Dog public house for a warm up and a lunch break. Then it was on to Barton, where we were collected by coach and taken to Stalham School for a nice hot meal, before meeting our students for the week. Pauline remembers this day with mixed feelings, being a non-swimmer and not at all that keen

140

on being on the water her best part was the hot dinner at Stalham! Mrs Slaughter, the school cook who looked after us all on those courses, has always been my treasured friend for all these years.

Early 1954 I had to go off into the Marines to do my National Service and from then on did no more instructing on the Broads. I did however get plenty of sailing when in Malta in 1955, teaching some of my marine mates and a couple of Wrens.

Lugsail halfdecker at Stokesby in Easter 1950. Keith Rackham.

We've had day boats out from Wroxham and Ludham to take trips to Ranworth and St Bennets, not however sailing, and we did borrow a sail boat owned by a friend. We have four daughters and seven grandchildren so I no longer do much on the river.

We did have a week during August 1987, with Pauline and our youngest, Lucy, on a Blueline cruiser from Horning. We covered the Bure from Belaugh to Great Yarmouth, with all the rivers and broads below Potter Heigham. The water was so high that week we would have lost about half a day waiting to go under the bridge with the pilot and all the other boats waiting. We did go to Oulton, Berney Arms and Reedham so the girls got a look at all my old haunts. We had an electric 'picnic boat' out for a day in August 2003, with 2 daughters, a friend and 3 grandchildren.

I have always loved the Broads, they have given me so many good times with many friends and my family. It has been a great pleasure to recall some of these things for Sheila to record. I need to say thank you for keeping my brain alive, and making me get all my photographs out to jog the memory. The pleasure has been all mine.

DRAINAGE BOARDS.

The present drainage boards covering most of these areas were set up in the 1930s and are:

Lower Bure, Halvergate Fleet & Acle Marshes, covering some 4.074 ha,
Middle Bure 2,033 ha, and Muckfleet & South Flegg 2,734 ha.

Earlier drainage commissions were established in the 19th century and include:

Upton & Fishley Drainage Commission set up in 1802.
Runham Drainage Commission in 1802,
Burgh & Billockoby Drainage Commission in 1801,
Muckfleet Improvement Drainage Committee in 1869,
Acle Marshes Drainage Authority in about 1861.

The Land Drainage Act of 1930 led to the establishment of the East Norfolk Rivers Catchment Board in 1931.

SOME LANDMARKS IN THE DEVELOPMENT OF DRAINAGE MILLS.

1745   Fantail invented by Edmund Lee.
1772   Parallel Shutters for windmill sails invented by Andrew Meicke.
1807   Patent Sails invented by William Cubitt.
1851   Turbine Pump invented by Appold.

WEAVER'S WAY.

The Weaver's way starts at Runham Vauxhall but follows the north side of Breydon Water as far as Berney Arms when it crosses the marshes going through Halvergate and then on towards the east side of Acle. The Weaver's Way then follows the River Bure for a short distance joining at Acle Dyke on the north side of the dyke, crossing the river at Acle Bridge and leaves the river at South Oby Dyke. It later follows the River Thurne at Thurne Dyke.

RIVER REACHES.

Stretches of the Bure were given names by the wherrymen who travelled along the river. The names usually related to the nearby facilities or buildings, or the people who lived nearby. Many of the reaches were marked on Hamilton's Maps.

Some of the Lower Bure River reaches starting from the Yarmouth end include:

Bowling Green Reach, probably named after the public house of that name near the mouth of the river.

North Quay

Sluice Reach.

Muckhole Reach.

Cinder Oven Reach, probably named after the Yarmouth Refuse Destructor.

Black House Reach named after Black House in 'Nowhere'.

Two Mile Steam Mill Reach

Black Mill Reach, named after Caister Black Mill

Three Mile House Reach

Scaregap

Four Mile Short and Long Reaches.

Five Mile Long Reach

Howe's Short Reach, named after the Howe family who lived near Runham Swim.

Dovehouse Reach, named after the nearby Dove House in Herringby.

Seven Mile House Reach, The Stacey Arms was originally Seven Mile House.

Black Mill Reach., probably named after the tarred black Old Hall Mill.

Tunstall Mill Reach

Tunstall Dyke Reach.

Stokesby Short Reach.

Stokesby Ferry Reach,

Trett's Mill Reach, named after the Trett family at Stokesby Cornmill.

Two Mills Reach, probably called this because of the Stokesby Commission Mill and the Calthorpe Level Mills being close together by the river.

Muckfleet Reach

Horseshoe Reach

Acle Bridge Reach.

Fishley Mill Reach.

Lower & Upper Davey's Reaches, named after the Davey family who were once marshmen at Clippesby Mill.

Oby Short Reach.

References and Bibliography

Mautby Remembrance, Samuel R. Howard, 1996, ISBN 1899758038
West Caister, Colin Tooke, 2004, ISBN0953295370
The Norfolk Broads: A landscape History, Tom Williamson, 1997, ISBN071904801X
The Norfolk Broads: A portrait in old picture postcards, Basil Gowen, 1990, ISBN1870708369
Drainage Windmills of the Norfolk Marshes, Arthur C. Smith, 1990, ISBN0951576607
Norfolk Windmills: Part II. Transactions of the Newcomen Soc. Rex Wailes, 1956.
A Broadseye View, Mike Page, 2005, ISBN1841144479
Great Yarmouth and Gorleston Pubs, Colin Tooke, 2004, ISBN0752432982
A History of Great Yarmouth, Frank Meeres, 2007, ISBN9781860772577
Time Gentlemen Please, Colin Tooke, 2006, ISBN 0953295397
An Acle Chronicle, Brian S. Grint, 1989, ISBN 9780946148394
A Diary of Great Yarmouth, John McBride, 1998, ISBN 0952071908
Norfolk's Windmills by river, road and rail, Luke Bonwick, 2008, ISBN 9780955631405

Many documents held at the Norfolk Records Office have been viewed and where the reference in the text begins NRO/ this refers to one of these documents.

Census Returns on microfilm have been examined at the Norwich Library.

Several White's, Kelly's and Harrod's directories of Norfolk and Great Yarmouth dating from 1836 held at Great Yarmouth Library, Norwich Library and the NRO have been consulted.

Licence Registers for Gt. Yarmouth NRO/Y/CJ31&32 and NRO/PS18/14/2, East & West Flegg NRO/PS17/4/1&2, and Blofield & Sth. Walsham NRO/PS8/6/1 to 4 have been examined.

The following Tithe Maps & Apportionments on microfilm at the NRO have been examined:

TUNSTALL Tithe Map & Apportionment NRO/MF 752.594 & MF777.594

ACLE Tithe Map & Apportionment NRO/MF747.1 & MF741.1

RUNHAM Tithe Map & Apportionment NRO/MF751.463 & MF772.463

STOKESBY Tithe Map & Apportionment NRO/MF752.527 & MF774.527

MAUTBY Tithe Map & Apportionment NRO/MF750.368 & MF768.368

ASHBY, OBY & THURNE Tithe Map & Apportionment NRO/MF747.13 & MF754.13

UPTON Tithe Map & Apportionment NRO/MF752.598 & MF777.598

FISHLEY Tithe Map & Apportionment NRO/MF749.209 & MF762.209

CANTLEY Tithe Map & Apportionment NRO/MF748.125 & MF758.125

CAISTER Tithe Map & Apportionment NRO/MF748.121 & MF758.12

YARMOUTH Tithe Map & Apportionment NRO/MF753.667 & MF780.667

BURGH ST. MARGARET Tithe Map & Apportionment NRO/MF748.107 & MF757.107

Acknowledgements.

The following are thanked for providing photographs and information, and for permission to include them in the book:

Peter Allard, David Childs, Brian Grint, Arnold Hewitt, John Lubbock, Mike Pickard, Keith Rackham, Arthur Smith, Colin Tooke, Derek Williams, Maurice Winter.

Special thanks go to Paul Hutchinson for his help with research, scanning of photographs, and typing the book for publication

Disclaimer

The information contained in this book has been collected from many old books, documents, maps and various individual's memories. The author has tried to check the accuracy of the information herein and apologises for any errors that may be present. The author cannot accept responsibility for any errors and omissions.

Other books by Sheila Hutchinson

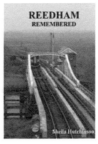

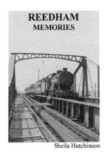

Berney Arms: Past & Present, 2000.

The Halvergate Fleet: Past & Present, 2001, ISBN0954168305

The Island (The Haddiscoe Island):Past & Present, 2002, ISBN0954168313.

Berney Arms Remembered, 2003, ISBN0954168321

Burgh Castle Remembered, 2005, ISBN095416833X

Reedham Remembered, 2006, ISBN0954168348

Reedham Memories, 2007, ISBN9780954168353.